Radio

GALS

Book, Music and Lyrics by

Mike Craver and Mark Hardwick

SAMUEL FRENCH, INC.
45 WEST 25TH STREET   NEW YORK 10010
7623 SUNSET BOULEVARD   HOLLYWOOD 90046
LONDON   TORONTO

RADIO GALS premiered at the Arkansas Repertory Theatre in Little Rock on March 18, 1993, directed by Cliff Fannin Baker, musical direction by Mark Hardwick, scenic design by Mike Nichols, sound design by Chip Salerno, costume design by Yslan Hicks, lighting design by Ken White, properties mistress Faith Farrell, choreography by Sally Riggs. Produced by the Arkansas Repertory Theatre in association with the Arkansas Power and Light Company.

HAZEL HUNT	Candyce Hinkle
GLADYS FRITTS	Vivian Morrison
RENNABELLE	Klea Blackhurst
AMERICA	Emily Mikesell
MISS MABEL SWINDLE	Mark Hardwick
MISS AZILEE SWINDLE	Mike Craver
O.B. ABBOTT	Joel Spineti

RADIO GALS was produced in New York by Elliot Martin & Ron Shapiro, in association with Marjorie Martin, Lee Mimms & Amick Byram. Directed by Marcia Milgrom Dodge, set design by Narelle Sissons, costume design by Michael Krass, lighting design by Joshua Starbuck, sound design by Tom Morse, musical supervision by Christopher Drobny, general management Ralph Roseman, public relations Jeffrey Richards, production stage manager Daniel Munson, casting by Pat McCorkle & Tim Sutton, musical arrangements by Mark Hardwick, with Klea Blackhurst, Mike Craver & Emily Mikesell. At the John Houseman Theatre, NYC, October 1, 1996.

HAZEL HUNT	Carole Cook
GLADYS FRITTS	Rosemary Loar
RENNABELLE	Klea Blackhurst
AMERICA	Emily Mikesell
MISS MABEL SWINDLE	Michael Rice
MISS AZILEE SWINDLE	Mike Craver
O.B. ABBOTT	Matthew Bennett

Part of the story for **RADIO GALS** was born from an actual incident in the life of evangelist Aimee Semple MacPherson, who ran a radio station out of her temple in Los Angeles. MacPherson was prone to "wavejumping": wandering from channel to channel through the ether in search of broadcast space that was "clear". This was in violation of Federal wavelength code and it wasn't long before Aimee's broadcasting efforts caught the attention of the Department of Commerce.

Herbert Hoover, then Secretary of Commerce, sent an inspector to seal MacPherson's station. MacPherson responded with an angry telegram to Hoover: "Please order your minions of Satan to leave my station alone. You cannot expect the Almighty to abide by your wavelength nonsense. When I offer my prayers to Him, I must fit into His wave reception. Open this station at once!"

It was rumored that Aimee Semple MacPherson then eloped with the inspector... on his motorcycle.

Although the setting for "Radio Gals" is rural, Hazel Hunt and her associates should not be portrayed as 'rubes' or 'yokels'. They are true 'eccentrics'. They are also intelligent and creative people, eager to use the new technology of radio to express themselves, even if they don't fully understand every aspect of it.

The Swindle Sisters have been traditionally played by men. These roles, however, shouldn't be treated as "drag". The Swindles are merely quiet, elderly, eccentric spinsters, perhaps with a "past" which is best kept secret.

Hazel Hunt and her Hazelnuts attempt to maintain a professional awareness of the radio microphone, and the fact that their activities in the parlor are being broadcast. Hazel, in particular, strives to address herself, and the activities of her company, to the radio audience at all times. Of course, in the heat of the moment this focus may be momentarily lost.

The action takes place on a warm spring day in the parlor of Hazel Hunt's home in Cedar Ridge, Arkansas. It is the late 1920's, well before "The Crash".

CHARACTERS

HAZEL HUNT: Retirement age, matronly. Shrewd, enthusiastic, perhaps a bit dotty, but definitely in control. Hazel is the town's beloved music teacher and patroness of the arts. (Voice: low female range.)

GLADYS FRITTS: Middle aged. More dramatic than Hazel: thin, high strung, and single. Gladys is a small town gal who yearns for greater horizons. She considers herself artistic and sophisticated. She possesses a deep love of poetry, and has studied voice. (Voice: lyric soprano.)

O. B. ABBOTT: Age 30's-40's. Bureaucratic, and self important, yet underneath Abbott has the soul of a poet. Abbott is a "closet" musician and singer. (Voice: tenor or light baritone. Accordion.)

AMERICA: Breezy, sunny, open, young woman. Unsophisticated, but enthusiastic. (Voice: soprano w/country belt. Violin, saxophone, clarinet, flute.)

RENNABELLE: America's cousin, perhaps a little older. Somewhat more tom-boyish, and "liberated". (Voice: alto, w/belt. Drums, trumpet.)

MISS AZILEE SWINDLE: Elderly lady, friend and associate of Hazel's. (Voice: tenor/light baritone w/falsetto. Upright bass, tuba, guitar.)

MISS MABEL SWINDLE: Sister of Azilee. Elderly lady, friend and associate of Hazel's. (Voice: tenor/baritone w/falsetto. Piano.)

MUSICAL NUMBERS

ACT I

"Sunrise Melody" ....HAZEL & THE HAZELNUTS
"Aviatrix Love Song"................. AMERICA& THE HAZELNUTS
"If Stars Could Talk" .....GLADYS, RENNABELLE & AMERICA
"When It's Sweetpea Time in Georgia" ....MISS AZILEE
"Dear Mr. Gershwin".. RENNABELLE
"The Tranquil Boxwood" ....GLADYS
"There are Fairies in My Mother's Flower Garden ....GLADYS
"A Fireside, A Pipe and A Pet" ...............................O.B. ABBOTT
"Edna Jones, the Elephant Girl".. ALL
"Paging the Ether/Play Gypsies Play" ....HAZEL & THE
                                                          HAZELNUTS

ACT II

"Royal Radio" ....AMERICA & THE HAZELNUTS
"Weather Song".. HAZELNUTS
"Buster He's A Hot Dog Now".... MISS MABEL & MISS AZILEE
"Why Did You Make Me Love You?" .....................O.B. ABBOTT
"Old Gals Are the Best Pals After All"................ HAZEL, AZILEE
                                                          & MABEL
"A Gal's Got To Do What A Gal's Got To Do" ....HAZEL
"Whispering Pines" ....ALL
"Wedding of the Flowers" ....ALL
"Queenie Take Me Home With You".. ALL

ACT I

(As the curtain rises, HAZEL comes bustling into the parlor. It is early morning and she is preparing for her daily broadcast. She may be finishing her cup of coffee, fiddling with her hair, & perhaps softly singing a verse of "The Wedding of the Flowers" [Song #34], as she turns on the transmitter. She positions herself before the microphone and speaks:)

HAZEL. Good morning, Glories. Welcome to WGAL, the radiophonic voice of Cedar Ridge, Arkansas. This is Hazel Hunt speaking. I have just come on the air and I am wondering if anyone is listening. How about you, Mr. Hitchcock? Have you slopped your hogs yet? And you, Miss Peach, poor thing! How's your irregularity? Remember what the Psalmist says: "Heaviness may endure for a night, but Joy cometh in the morning!" Doc Gump, I know you're listening... Look in on Miss Peach, will you. By the way, I'm simply wild about your new paling fence! Am I coming through loud and clear, Dear Hearts? Ring me up on the Royal Telephone and tell me if I am. That's Katydid 23. And I certainly hope you'll enjoy the program. *(There is a knock at the front door. HAZEL smiles.)* Well, I declare, it seems as though we have visitors. *(The front door opens and the HAZELNUTS—AMERICA, RENNABELLE, MISS MABEL and MISS AZILEE—enter.)* Come in, lambs. *(HAZEL waves them in.)* If it isn't my Hazelnuts. Morning, glories!

HAZELNUTS. (Singing: #1.)
GOOD MORNING, HAZEL.

(The HAZELNUTS bustle to their places, carrying handbags, sheet music, etc.; AMERICA carrying a jar of mayonnaise, as HAZEL introduces them:)

HAZEL. My Hazelnuts. I'd like you all to meet them. Here's Miss Azilee and Miss Mabel Swindle. Trusty and true, fellow Sisters of Pythias—AND dedicated baseball fans! How about those Cedar Ridge Yellow Hammers, girls?

MISS MABEL and MISS AZILEE. Woo!

HAZEL. And looky, here's Rennabelle and America. Girls, how are we this morning?

AMERICA. Fresh as daisies.

RENNABELLE. Not me. Spent all Sunday making mayonnaise.

AMERICA. It was fun!

HAZEL. That fancy new sauce I've been reading so much about. What will they think of next?

AMERICA. *(Holding up the jar of mayonnaise.)* It's the latest thing. Ended up gallons of the stuff.

RENNABELLE. What are we going to do with all that goo?

HAZEL. Why, make Waldorf Salad. Tubs of it!

RENNABELLE. Hazel, you're a Solomon!

HAZEL. Poppycock! Has anybody seen Gladys?

RENNABELLE. She stopped by the Post Office.

AMERICA. She'll be along directly.

HAZEL. Flirting with the mailmen again. When is she gonna come down from her pink balloon. My Hazelnuts... well, almost all of 'em! Life's been peaches since we've been together.

RENNABELLE. There hasn't been a silent night in Cedar Ridge for months.

HAZEL. *(Raising her arm like a coach signaling a footrace to begin.)* And with the help of God and my Western Electric Five Hundred Watt Radio Transmitter, there won't ever be!

(HAZEL chops the air, giving AMERICA the go.)

AMERICA. This is...

HAZELNUTS. (Singing #2:)
WGAL
IN CEDAR RIDGE,
ARKANSAS.

HAZEL. Wake up, Cedar Ridge. I want to hear the whole town singing!

(RENNABELLE makes a rooster crow noise, then the HAZELNUTS
start the song with HAZEL conducting:)

#3 "SUNRISE MELODY"

HAZELNUTS.
TIME'S A-FLYING
DEW'S A-TWINKLING
BACON'S FRYING
CHINA'S TINKLING
GLORY, IT'S A SUNRISE MELODY.

WIPE THE SLEEP FROM YOUR EYES.
NOW'S THE TIME TO HARMONIZE.
GLORY, IT'S A SUNRISE MELODY.
RENNABELLE.
EVERY COW THAT'S MOOING
SEEMS TO SAY WAKE UP
SWINDLES.
WAKE UP!
RENNABELLE.
SMELL THAT COFFEE BREWING.
HAZELNUTS.
WOULDN'T YOU LIKE A GREAT BIG CUP?

BUGS ARE BUZZING
BREEZES BLOWING
FIDO'S BARKING
LET'S GET GOING
GLORY, IT'S A SUNRISE MELODY, DE DE DE DE
GLORY, IT'S A SUNRISE MELODY MELODY MELODY

HAZEL.
MAMA'S BUSY SCRAMBLING
EGGS FOR EVERYONE
HEAR THAT FIDDLE PLAYING
ALL.
COME ON, BOYS, LET'S HAVE SOME FUN.

HAZEL & HAZELNUTS.
WHAT'S THAT MUSIC IN THE TREES?
IS IT BIRDIES? IS BEES?
GLORY, IT'S A SUNRISE MELODY, DE DE DE DE
GLORY, IT'S A SUNRISE MELODY MELODY MELODY

HAZEL. If that didn't wake you up, I don't know what will. *(The phone rings, HAZEL answers it.)* Hello, WGAL!... Mr. Hitchcock! Say what? We're fading out and you're picking up the Paragould Farm report? Drat! *(HAZEL runs over to the transmitter.)* Clear channels are as scarce as hen's teeth these days. *(She fiddles with dials.)* Dear Hearts, we're going to the left today. Now everyone be sure and follow—one full turn. *(She turns the dial.)* That should do nicely. *(Into the telephone.)* How's this, Mr. Hitchcock?

HAZELNUTS. (Singing #4:)
TESTING, TESTING
ONE, TWO, THREE

HAZEL. *(Listening to the telephone, then saying to the girls.)* He says we're coming in clear as a bell. *(Into the telephone.)* Is your brood sow feelin' better? *(Giggling, to girls.)* He says Petunia perks up every time she hears America sing. *(Into the telephone.)* Ezra, you old wag! *(To the girls.)* I have a feeling Mr. Hitchcock perks up too!

AMERICA. I'll sing him something.

HAZEL. Oh Goody!

AMERICA. *(Into the microphone.)* I'd like to dedicate this song to my cousin Dorcas. She's starting a new county job today. She's going to be a crop duster!

HAZEL. Get out your helmet and goggles, Cedar Ridge, we're taking you all for a ride!

#5 "AVIATRIX LOVE SONG"

AMERICA.
SOME GALS LIKE TO BOB THEIR HAIR
AND GUZZLE BATHTUB GIN,
BUT I JUST CRANK MY JENNIE UP
AND TAKE HER FOR A SPIN.

THOSE FLAPPERS HAVE THEIR SILKEN HOSE
AND FLAGPOLE SITTIN' FELLERS.
JUST TOP ME OFF WITH KEROSENE
AND CRANK UP MY PROPELLERS.

AMERICA, with RENNABELLE, AZILEE and HAZEL.
OH, LET ME BE UP IN THE AIR
A–FLYIN', FLYIN', FLYIN'
WAY UP IN THE SUNNY SUNNY BLUE.
OH, CAN'T YOU HEAR MY LITTLE ENGINES
HUMMIN', HUMMIN', HUMMIN'
AN AVIATRIX LOVE SONG JUST FOR YOU.

AMERICA.
YO–DE LAY OH DE LAY EE
YO–DE LAY OH DE LAY EE
YOD–E LAY EE
YOD–E LAY EE
YOD–E LAY EE HOO

*(We hear the barking of a dog offstage toward the end of the yodels.
In the turnaround, HAZEL runs to the door and yells "HUSH UP
OUT THERE!")*

AMERICA.
SOME GALS LIKE TO FOX-TROT
AND TWO-STEP 'TIL THEY'RE BEAT,
BUT ME I CHARLESTON ON THE WING
AT SEVEN THOUSAND FEET.

THEY SAY THE SKY'S THE LIMIT,
BUT IF I TAKE A NOTION,
ONE DAY I MIGHT JUST ZIP ACROSS
THAT GREAT ATLANTIC OCEAN.

AMERICA and RENNABELLE.
YO–DE LAY OH DE LAY EE
YO–DE LAY OH DE LAY EE

YOD–E LAY EE
YOD–E LAY EE
YOD–E LAY EE
YOD–E LAY EE HOO

(Double-time.)
YO–DE LAY OH DE LAY EE
YO–DE LAY OH DE LAY EE
YOD–E LAY EE
YOD–E LAY EE
YOD–E LAY EE
YOD–E LAY
YOD–E LAY EE
YOD–E LAY EE
YOD–E LAY EE
YOD–E LAY
YOD–E LAY EE
YOD–E LAY EE
YOD–E LAY EE
YOD–E LAY EE HOO

HAZEL. Merciful Heavens, that was so much fun I feel down-right dizzy! *(Reading from a card.)* Now don't forget, Dear Hearts, Doc May and His Musical Goats will be appearing up at Lake Kitchykoo Lodge this Saturday Night. Ya'll know how popular those Musical Goats are. It's one night only, so get your tickets early.

(GLADYS enters, carrying a paper bag and some letters.)

GLADYS. Hello, my Darlings!

The HAZELNUTS play #6A: "Gladys' Entrance"

HAZEL. Well, look who danced through the door—if it isn't Miss Gladys Fritts, the voice of the Lowlands. Mornin' glory.
HAZELNUTS *(Singing #6B.)*
GOOD MORNING, GLADYS.
GLADYS. Sorry I'm late. I was reading the Postmaster's palm. He has the nicest hands!

HAZEL. Gladys is our resident Travel Hostess, Gourmand and Seer. We refer to her affectionately as Swami G. *(To GLADYS.)* O Mystic One, where will you be taking us later this morning?

GLADYS. Darkest Africa!

RENNABELLE. Did you bring the sandwiches?

GLADYS. *(Holding up paper bag.)* Mais out!

AMERICA. What kind?

GLADYS. Cream cheese and olives for you girls. *(Sighing.)* Stewed prunes for me.

HAZEL. Oh, dear! Indigestion again? *(MISS AZILEE, who has been polishing the tuba and blowing out its valves, inadvertently makes a short, flatulent-sounding noise.)* I've got just the thing. *(HAZEL holds up a bottle of Horehound Compound.)* Hunt's Horehound Compound! Are you troubled by dyspepsia, flatulence, or agues? Just one bottle of Hunt's Amazing elixir of Horehound and many of these ailments will cease! Hazelnuts?

#7: "HOREHOUND COMPOUND #1"

AMERICA, RENNABELLE, AZILEE, MABEL & GLADYS.
HOREHOUND COMPOUND
IT'S THE LATEST STUFF
STRONGER THAN MEDICINE
CLEANER THAN SNUFF
SECRET HERBS AND JUNGLE JUICES
GOOD FOR ABOUT A THOUSAND USES
HOREHOUND COMPOUND IT'S THE STUFF

HAZEL. From an old family recipe handed down from Grandpa Hunt. It's almost ten years since he crossed the swelling tide. How time marches on. I'll be pickin' a washtub full of lilacs to put on his grave next Sunday.

GLADYS. *(Holding up a handful of letters.)* Hazel, would you look at these letters!

HAZEL. Oh, Goody. It's time for "Listener Mail"

MISS MABEL and MISS AZILEE begin #8: "Mail Bag Rag" underscoring.

GLADYS. Here's one from Magnolia...

AMERICA. *(Holding up another envelope.)* Eureka Springs...

RENNABELLE. *(Holding up another envelope, & whistling.)* This one's all the way from Arkadelphia: "We'd be ever so grateful for a souvenir photograph of Hazel Hunt," signed the Hutchinsons, Rural Route Three."

HAZEL. What would a body want with such foolishness. *(HAZEL gets up to go search the shelves.)* I believe I've got some extras around here somewhere.

GLADYS. *(Thumbing through more mail.)* 'Petty Jean Mountain', Calico Rock, De Valls Bluff... Such faraway places! Hazel, we're like a beacon, beaming o'er the mighty ocean of Ether: that wondrous radio phonic essence bearing up in its magnificent tide the very stars and planets of all Creation.

HAZEL. She's talking about air, Dear Hearts.

RENNABELLE. *(Picking up another letter.)* Uh oh, Hazel, here's another letter from old Mr. Couch over at WBTM in Paragould. "Dear Miss Hunt, yesterday, during our Farm News program, I suddenly and distinctly heard the raucous tones of your orchestra... again. You leave me no alternative but to complain to the authorities." Hazel, this sounds serious.

HAZEL. I'm not afraid of Old Mr. Couch. I'll send over a case of Horehound compound. That'll salve his wounds.

GLADYS. I wish I had something for mine. I passed a most troublesome eve. The strangest dreams. Sheiks in sports cars, appliance salesmen on motorcycles...

HAZEL. Men, again? You've been watching too many moving pictures, honey. You know how susceptible you are. *(Aside, to AMERICA.)* America, fetch the Gazette. *(To microphone.)* Dear Hearts, it's time to consult the sign.

(AMERICA gets the newspaper while GLADYS puts on her turban.)

HAZEL. Love the turban.

GLADYS. Made it from a Vogue pattern.

HAZEL. She looks stunning, doesn't she, girls?

HAZELNUTS. You do, you do.

GLADYS. It's a miracle of the rouge pot and face powder!

(AMERICA gives GLADYS the GAZETTE.)

HAZEL. How now, Swami G.

#9: "IF STARS COULD TALK"

AMERICA, GLADYS, RENNABELLE.
IF STARS COULD TALK IMAGINE WHAT THEY'D SAY
ABOUT THE SECRETS OF THE MILKY WAY
DO YOU THINK THEY COMPLAIN BECAUSE THEY HAVE
      TO GLOW
THERE'S NOTHING THAT THE STARS DON'T KNOW.
    GLADYS. I am pouring o'er the celestial realms. The Heavens shall reveal enchantments and sorceries. Dare ye list' to the mystic cipher?
    AMERICA/RENNABELLE. We're all ears.
    GLADYS. *(Reading the GAZETTE.)* Let's see, Monday the 18th. Sagittarius... "You have a flair for the dramatic." *(To the girls.)* Do you think so?
    HAZELNUTS. You do, you do.
    GLADYS. *(Reading.)* "You will soon take a trip and feel the wind in your wings!"
    AMERICA. Can I go too?
    GLADYS. Silly girl! *(Reading.)* Listen to this. "Beware of a tall dark stranger singing love songs. He will steal your heart away!"
    RENNABELLE. Not much chance of that around here.
    GLADYS. Oh Hazel, I'm all a-twitter.
    HAZEL. Steady honey, you've got a full day of broadcasting ahead of you.

(Suddenly from outside, there is the sound of a motorcycle approaching.)

    GLADYS. Hark!
    HAZEL. Goodness, what could that be?
    AMERICA. *(Looking out the window.)* It's a man!

(GLADYS gives an anguished cry & faints—spread-eagle, with feet pointing downstage—on the floor.)

ALL. A man?

(HAZEL & SWINDLES rush over and push GLADYS' legs together. RENNABELLE rushes to the window to see.)

HAZEL. Somebody fetch the smelling salts. *(One of the SWINDLES fetches the smelling salts. HAZEL says to GLADYS.)* Honey, are you alright?

(One of the SWINDLES puts the smelling salts under GLADYS' nose.)

HAZEL. It's probably just another tenor, wanting to audition.
RENNABELLE. I'll bet he sings "I Love You Truly"!
HAZEL. Don't they all.
GLADYS. *(Reviving.)* Is he tall dark and handsome?
AMERICA. Well, he's breathing.

(GLADYS moans and swoons again.)

RENNABELLE. He's awful serious looking...
HAZEL. *(Holding her hand over the microphone so her listeners won't hear.)* It could be a revenue officer! *(To the SWINDLES.)* Run out and throw a quilt over the still.

(MABEL and AZILEE exit, as we hear someone knocking at the front door.)

HAZEL. *(Loudly into microphone.)* Dear Hearts! It seems as though we have a visitor!

(HAZEL opens the door to find O.B. ABBOTT standing there. He is carrying a briefcase.)

ABBOTT. Hazel Hunt?
HAZEL. Speaking.
ABBOTT. O.B. Abbott's the name. I have some important business to discuss with you.
HAZEL. I know, I know... your career! Do come in. *(Introducing*

the others.) These are my assistants, America and Rennabelle... and this is my associate, Miss Gladys Fritts.

GLADYS. *(Dreamily, to ABBOTT.)* Are you a tenor?

HAZEL. *(Soothing GLADYS.)* Shh, honey!

ABBOTT. Is she okay?

HAZEL. She'll be fine. She's just a little excitable.

(AMERICA and RENNABELLE help GLADYS up as AZILEE & MABEL re-enter. ABBOTT looks them up and down.)

HAZEL. And these are my dearest and oldest friends, Miss Mabel and Miss Azilee...

ABBOTT. *(To SWINDLES.)* Haven't we met before?

HAZEL. *(Directing the SWINDLES away from ABBOTT.)* It's a wide world. A body could get confused. Just give your music to Miss Mabel, she can sight read anything.

ABBOTT. Sight read. But I don't...

HAZEL. You don't? Well, neither does Miss Azilee—poor thing—can't read a note. But she's still a local favorite. *(HAZEL beckons for AZILEE to come forward, then to ABBOTT.)* Wait till you hear her! *(Into microphone.)* Get out your handkerchiefs, Cedar Ridge, Miss Azilee's going to sing one of her heart songs.

(AZILEE comes forward with guitar.)

ABBOTT. You're on the air now?

HAZEL. Whatever, whenever, however—that's our motto.

#10: "WHEN IT'S SWEETPEA TIME IN GEORGIA"

MISS AZILEE.
WHEN IT'S SWEETPEA TIME IN GEORGIA
I'LL BE THINKING, DEAR, OF YOU—
IN THE GOLDEN LIGHT OF MORNING
WE'D PICK SWEETPEAS IN THE DEW

'TWAS THERE YOU TOLD ME THAT YOU LOVED ME
AND FOREVER WOULD BE TRUE

WE'D WALK HAND IN HAND TOGETHER
DOWN LIFE'S CROWDED AVENUE

THEN ONE DAY I GOT A LETTER
IN AN ENVELOPE OF BLUE
YOU TOLD ME THAT YOU LOVED ANOTHER
AND NO LONGER COULD BE TRUE

WITH AMERICA & RENNABELLE HUMMING.
IF IT HAD BEEN SOME GREAT BEAUTY
I COULD UNDERSTAND YOUR HEART
OR ONE WITH LOTS OF GOLD AND SILVER
FOR GOLD AND SILVER PLAY A PART
AZILEE. (Solo.)
BUT YOU SAID YOU'D ALWAYS LOVED ANOTHER
ONE WITH SILV'RY LOCKS OF HAIR
'TWAS NONE OTHER THAN YOUR MOTHER
AND, MY DEAR, I COULD NOT BEAR

(INSTRUMENTAL BREAK)

AZILEE. (Cont.)
WHEN IT'S SWEETPEA TIME IN GEORGIA
I NO LONGER THINK OF YOU
I DECIDED TO PLANT PEANUTS
AND TO PEANUTS I'LL BE TRUE.
HAZEL. *(To ABBOTT.)* She's had a pretty hard time of it, Mr. Abbott. *(To AZILEE.)* No one ever said it would be a crystal stair-case, dear. *(To ABBOTT.)* Now, about your "problem" here—let me take a look at your repertoire.

(HAZEL reaches for ABBOTT's briefcase.)

ABBOTT. I don't have a repertoire—I'm from the Department of Commerce—Radio Division—Fifth District, to be exact. I've been sent here to observe your broadcasting procedures.
HAZEL. Broadcasting procedures? We'd be honored, wouldn't we, girls?

ABBOTT. If you don't mind, I'd like to ask you a few questions.

HAZEL. Go ahead, Mr. Abbott. My life is an open book. Mind you, don't dog-ear the pages.

(The HAZELNUTS are amused by HAZEL's remark. ABBOTT isn't.)

ABBOTT. First of all—how did you ever become a broadcaster?

HAZEL. Well, I'd been teaching music here in Cedar Ridge since I was younger than America.

RENNABELLE. Hazel won the Euterpe Medal of Honor thirty years running...

HAZEL. Ah, the world and all it's baubles! My arthritis got so bad two years ago I had to call it quits.

AMERICA. The whole town was sick about it.

RENNABELLE. We all got together and gave Hazel the nicest retirement party.

HAZEL. Every snaggle toothed kid in town was there. Not to mention all the civic organizations—

RENNABELLE. The Lions...

AMERICA. The Elks...

HAZEL. The Loyal Order of the Horned Larks.

GLADYS. The Mayor made the floweriest speech.

HAZEL. "Hazel Hunt," he said, "you've been an inspiration to the youth of Cedar Ridge. Now go forth and gussy up all of Central Arkansas."

RENNABELLE. Then the boys wheeled up this great big crate.

AMERICA. At first Hazel thought it was an electric washing machine.

HAZEL. *(Chuckling.)* Oh that's right, I did. But when the boys got out their crowbars and pried that thing open... there she was! *(Pointing to the transmitter.)* A brand new Western Electric Five Hundred Watt Radio Transmitter!

GLADYS. *(Gazing at ABBOTT.)* It was love at first sight!

HAZEL. Sometimes I wish it had been an electric washing machine. I'd be happy. Just the two of us and a box of Oxydol. But that's all water down the drain now!

(Again, the other LADIES are amused by HAZEL's remark. ABBOTT isn't.)

ABBOTT. *(Inspecting the transmitter.)* Well, at least it looks like it's up to code.

HAZEL. Oh, it's up to code. The Mayor gave us a license. I've got it framed.

RENNABELLE. *(Proudly straightening up the framed license which is hanging on the wall.)* It's signed by the Secretary of Commerce himself...

ABBOTT. Mr. Herbert Hoover!

HAZEL. You know him?

ABBOTT. He's my boss!

GLADYS. What's he really like?

HAZEL. *(Directing ABBOTT to the microphone.)* Do tell the Dear Hearts, Mr. Abbott...

ABBOTT. *(Nervously leaning toward the microphone.)* Well, ah, I've never really spent a lot of time around him... on a one to one basis. He's a very busy man. *(GLADYS and the HAZELNUTS sigh in disappointment. Sensing this, ABBOTT adds.)* But he's promised to have me and the boys over for a game of pinochle next month.

(GLADYS and the HAZELNUTS are impressed. HAZEL isn't.)

GLADYS. You don't say!

ABBOTT. *(Recalling himself to the task at hand.)* Now, Miss Hunt, exactly how did you acquire you... radio orchestra?

HAZEL. Well, I couldn't very well broadcast all by myself. So I put out an SOS for talent and guess who showed up?

HAZELNUTS. We did!

HAZEL. All my star pupils.

GLADYS. The entire local chapter of the Sisters of Pythias.

(The LADIES all proudly indicate their Sisters of Pythias brooches.)

HAZEL. And what a tub full of talent it was! I couldn't do without my Hazelnuts! *(HAZEL singles out each member.)* Rennabelle here, she's my head. America's my heart. Miss Azilee and Miss Mabel are my hands. And Gladys is my—*(To ABBOTT.)* I digress, Mr. Abbott. Suffice it to say that every radio station worth its salt needs a Masked Soprano.

GLADYS. *(Flattered.)* Oh Hazel!

HAZEL. So, you might say that's how the Hazelnuts were cracked. And there's not a walnut in the bunch.

(Once again, the other LADIES are amused by HAZEL's remark. ABBOTT, taking copious notes, isn't.)

ABBOTT. Now, Miss Hunt, if it wouldn't discommode you, I'd like to see your books.

HAZEL. Funny you should mention it. I've just gotten a leather-bound set of Fenimore Cooper!

ABBOTT. No. I mean your radio logs.

HAZEL. Radio logs? All I've got is a scrapbook. You're welcome to see it. *(Gesturing to AMERICA.)* America, be a lamb.

(AMERICA gets the scrapbook from a shelf and brings it to HAZEL. Everyone gathers around.)

ABBOTT. Does it contain all your air dates and running times?

HAZEL. No, it's mostly recipes and snapshots and things. Got all the big stars when they'd come through Little Rock. *(HAZEL opens it to an item of interest.)* Well, my goodness!

ABBOTT. What's that?

HAZEL. Rennabelle, here's that snapshot you took of Mr. Gershwin.

ABBOTT. That's George Gershwin?

RENNABELLE. It's just the side of his head. It's a little blurry—I was nervous when I took it.

ABBOTT. You know him?

RENNABELLE. Oh yeah.

HAZEL. Last fall, Mr. Gershwin gave a concert at the Masonic Temple in Pine Bluff. Rennabelle was the Hospitality Committee.

RENNABELLE. I fixed the sandwiches.

GLADYS. She's never gotten over it.

HAZEL. *(Confidentially to ABBOTT.)* It took Mr. Gershwin a while too.

RENNABELLE. He was a finicky eater.

AMERICA. Rennabelle wrote a song about it.

RENNABELLE. Hush, America.

HAZEL. Wait 'till you hear her sing.

ABBOTT. *(Holding up his pad and pencil.)* But my investigation...

HAZEL. She's the Volunteer Fire Department's favorite.

11: "DEAR MR. GERSHWIN"

RENNABELLE.
DEAR MR. GERSHWIN,
YOU MAY NOT REMEMBER ME,
THE GIRL FROM HOSPITALITY.
I HELPED YOU ORDER YOUR LUNCH.
MR. GERSHWIN,
DID I TURN YOUR HEAD
WHEN I SAID "WHAT KIND OF BREAD
WOULD YOU LIKE
ON YOUR HAM AND CHEESE?
WOULD YOU LIKE WHITE?"
YOU SAID YOU MIGHT LIKE RYE,
SO I SAID "WHY?"
THEN YOU SAID "WHY NOT?"
WHAT COULD I SAY BUT
"I'VE GOT WHEAT, MR. GERSHWIN.
SWEET MR. GERSHWIN,
WHEAT IS ALL I'VE GOT FOR YOU."

DEAR MR. GERSHWIN,
RIGHT AFTER DINNER
YOU LOOKED EVEN THINNER TO ME.
I COULD TELL YOU'D BEEN TOO BUSY MAKING UP
MORE OF YOUR MELODIES
HOW COULD SOMEBODY LIKE ME
DARE TO INTERRUPT?
DEAR MR. GERSHWIN,
AT LEAST HAVE SOME CAKE.

HOW CAN YOU PLAY YOUR RHAPSODY RIGHT
WHEN YOU HAVEN'T TOUCHED A SINGLE BITE?
SOME MEAT, MR. GERSHWIN?
A BEET, MR. GERSHWIN?
BEETS ARE VERY GOOD FOR YOU.

*(During the instrumental break, RENNABELLE does a tap dance.
For the benefit of the listeners, HAZEL points the microphone
toward RENNABELLE's feet.)*

DEAR MR. GERSHWIN,
I SAW YOU THIS EVENING
AS YOU WERE LEAVING.
YOUR SUIT
WAS A MASTERPIECE.
WHEN YOU WERE STEPPING INTO YOUR LIMOUSINE,
I THREW A TANGERINE.
I THOUGHT YOU NEEDED FRUIT.
WHY WERE YOU STARING
OUT INTO SPACE?
THE LOOK ON YOUR FACE
WAS EVER SO ODD TO ME.,
WAS IT HUNGER OR GRIEF?
OR JUST PLAIN RELIEF?
MR. GERSHWIN, WHAT DID YOU SEE?
AN AMERICAN IN PARIS *(Pronounced "PAREE")*
A FLYING SAUCER OR A PRETTIER GIRL THAN ME?
DEAR MR. GERSHWIN AND ME.

HAZEL. So you can see, Mr. Abbott, we here at WGAL appreci-
ate all kinds of music, even the modern variety. Of course, nothing
compares with the immortal masters, like Bach, Beethoven—
GLADYS. Don't forget the Reverend Everhart!
ABBOTT. Who's he?
HAZEL. Gladys' "spiritual master".
AMERICA. A kindly old gent.
RENNABELLE. An odd fellow.

(ABBOTT is writing this all down.)

GLADYS. *(Defensively.)* And one of the state's most beloved composers. Why, everyone's familiar with "The Tranquil Boxwood."

#12: "THE TRANQUIL BOXWOOD"

GLADYS.
OFT TIMES IN EVENING'S DISMAL GLOOM,
I GAZE FAR FROM MY CLOISTERED ROOM
AND SEE BEYOND THE WORLD'S HUBBUB
MY TRANQUIL BOXWOOD IN ITS TUB.
BEHOLD YON BEAUTEOUS SHRUB!

ABBOTT. Spooky. *(ABBOTT closes his notebook and stands.)* Now...

GLADYS. How fondly I recall that old Bungalow on State Street, and the many pleasant afternoons I'd spend with the Reverend, under the China berry tree. I remember one spring afternoon in particular... we'd been weeding the marigolds, when suddenly the Reverends's eyes began shining with an otherworldly light. "Gladys, my child," he said to me, "I've had a vision." Then he dropped his trowel, gazed heavenward, and sang, note for note—this next song. Surely, Mr. Abbott, you recall these immortal strains.

(GLADYS folds her arms across her breast, palms on shoulders, and poses dramatically.)

13: "FAIRIES IN MY MOTHER'S FLOWER GARDEN"

GLADYS.
THERE ARE FAIRIES IN MY MOTHER'S FLOWER GARDEN;
I SAW THEM THROUGH MY WINDOWPANE LAST NIGHT.
THEY WERE DANCING ON THE LEAVES
AND GIGGLING IN THEIR SLEEVES,
AND THIS IS WHAT THEY SAID TO ME:

OO—OO—OO (*"OO" pronounced to rhyme with "You")

WE ARE THE FAIRIES,
OO—OO—OO *
FROM FAR AWAY.
OH, LEAVE YOUR HAPPY HOME,
AND COME WITH US TO ROAM
ALL THROUGH THE NIGHT UNTIL THE DAY,

(MUSIC BREAK)

THEY SAILED ME IN A SILVER SHIP OF MOONBEAMS
FAR ACROSS THE EVENING SKY,
AND THEN THE FAIRY KING,
HE BEAT HIS LITTLE WING,
AND AS HE FLEW AWAY I HEARD HIM CRY:

OO—OO—OO *
WE ARE THE FAIRIES,
OO—OO—OO *
FROM FAR AWAY
OH, LEAVE YOUR HAPPY HOME
AND COME WITH US TO ROAM
ALL THROUGH THE NIGHT UNTIL THE DAY

ABBOTT. It's a lovely song.

GLADYS. It's a true story. Of course it wasn't really a silver ship of moonbeams—it was a Copperhead Ford with a gutted muffler. The fairies were the strangest creatures. They had gold teeth. They forced the Reverend to drink spirits, and escorted him to the American Legion Hut, where they rumpled his hat, disconcerted his bowtie and strongly encouraged him to do an Apache Dance. I'm afraid the Reverend was never quite the same after that.

HAZEL. Can you imagine. A man of Reverend Everhart's dignity and bearing. What's the world coming to?

ABBOTT. You've certainly got a point there, sister. It's not the same old candy store it used to be. Fairies, eh? Sounds like Gypsies to me.

RENNABELLE. Gypsies!?

HAZELNUTS. (Singing # 14.)
PLAY GYPSIES PLAY,
MAKE THE MUSIC FAST...

(HAZEL, embarrassed, cuts them off.)

ABBOTT. Or worse—anarchists!

HAZEL. In Cedar Ridge?

ABBOTT. You can't be too sure about anyone anymore. I'm reminded of that case up in Chicago. Couple of Bluestocking suffragettes operatin' a two bit radio station out of their attic. Had an upright piano and a pump organ. Their big hit was the "Tennessee Tickle". Maybe you heard it? *(The LADIES all shake their heads and murmur "NO".)* Trouble was, in between rags they were channel jumping and pumping the ether full of free thinking propaganda. *(Suspiciously, to HAZEL.)* You got an attic?

HAZEL. Why, of course.

AMERICA. It's where Miss Gladys meditates.

ABBOTT. Meditates?

(ABBOTT scribbles this down on his notepad.)

GLADYS. The attic, I find, is particularly permeated with the electro-magnetic vibrations of Divine Will.

ABBOTT. *(Noting this.)* Divine will, eh?

GLADYS. It can move mountains. It can change the course of our destinies. Why, Divine Will has even brought you to Cedar Ridge! *(Advancing closer to ABBOTT.)* It's a lovely attic! Would you care to see?

ABBOTT. *(Looking GLADYS up and down.)* Maybe a little later. *(To HAZEL.)* Right now, I need to get down to brass tacks. And I'll be frank about it.

HAZEL. By all mean, Mr. Abbott. *(Recalling him to the radio audience.)* We here at WGAL insist upon honesty.

ABBOTT. As a matter of fact, my department has received a number of complaints about your station.

RENNABELLE & AMERICA. Complaints?

ABBOTT. Workmen have been receiving your signal in a tunnel under the Hudson River outside New York City.

(The LADIES squeal with delight.)

HAZEL. *(Proudly.)* Did you hear that, Cedar Ridge?

ABBOTT. And a lady in Santa Barbara California picked up your call letters in her frying pan while she was stirring beans.

AMERICA. Beans? Do tell!

ABBOTT. *(Looking suspiciously toward the transmitter.)* What wavelength are you on any way?

HAZEL. Wavelength?

AMERICA. What's that?

ABBOTT. Your engineer should know.

RENNABELLE. We don't have an engineer.

HAZEL. Mr. Hitchcock comes over once a week and goes over everything with sewing machine oil.

ABBOTT. Hitchcock, eh? Is he certified?

AMERICA. He's a pig farmer.

ABBOTT. *(Testily.)* I'm afraid that wouldn't cut much mustard with the Review Board!

HAZEL. *(Annoyed.)* Mr. Abbott, there is absolutely no need to bellow.

GLADYS. *(Mildly.)* Mr. Abbott, would you care for some coffee?

RENNABELLE. Or perhaps a cream cheese and olive sandwich?

(ABBOTT makes a face and shakes his head.)

AMERICA. We could put some mayonnaise on that.

ABBOTT. No thanks. *(ABBOTT's gaze rests on the Horehound display. He picks up a bottle of Horehound Compound and looks at it curiously.)* What's this stuff?

HAZEL. Horehound Compound.

ABBOTT. *(Uncorking a bottle, sniffing it and whistling.)* Banana crackers!

HAZEL. An old family recipe. Kept Grandpa Hunt from freezing to death during the Great War for Southern Independence.

(The LADIES all take a beat of silence with their heads lowered and their right hands over their hearts. ABBOTT takes a swig and chokes, much to the ladies' amusement.)

ABBOTT. Tastes like gin to me.

HAZEL. *(Covering the microphone with her hand.)* Mr. Abbott, a radio station has to run on more than Delco batteries. Hazelnuts?

 # 15: "HOREHOUND #2"

AMERICA, RENNABELLE, AZILEE, MABEL & GLADYS.
HOREHOUND COMPOUND, GOOD FOR ALL YOUR NEEDS,
BRIGHTENS YOUR ATTITUDE
GETS RID OF WEEDS.
GOES DOWN EASY NEVER SCORCHES
TAKES THE PAINT OFF
CHAIRS AND PORCHES
HOREHOUND COMPOUND, IT'S THE STUFF.

HAZEL. That's right, just twenty cents. Come on by the house and pick up your bottle today.

ABBOTT. Miss Hunt, this is bald faced hucksterism.

HAZEL. It's a beautiful thing, isn't it?

ABBOTT. I'll have you know there's a Constitutional Amendment prohibiting the production and sale of...

HAZEL. Excuse me, Mr. Abbott, but would you mind terribly if the Swami *(Indicating GLADYS.)* took a look at your hand?

ABBOTT. Swami?

(GLADYS has slipped on her turban, takes ABBOTT's hand, and studies his palm.)

HAZEL. Oh yes, she's had a correspondence course.

GLADYS. Observe his Girdle of Venus!

HAZEL. Not bad. What about his Sword of Apollo?

GLADYS. It's huge! *(To ABBOTT.)* Mr. Abbott, you MAY possess a gift for music.

ABBOTT. Me?

RENNABELLE. It's Hazel's theory that everyone has talent.

AMERICA. Even government people.

ABBOTT. Well, I used to play a little accordion...

GLADYS. Noble savage.

ABBOTT. Father never approved. "A true gentleman," he used to say, "is one who knows how to play the accordion... but won't."

HAZEL. I'll have you know my Grandpa Hunt played the accordion—quite well, as a matter of fact. And he was every bit a gentleman. *(Reverently pointing to Grandpa Hunt's accordion which hangs on the wall.)* Yonder's his old squeeze box.

AMERICA. Genuine Italian.

RENNABELLE. Mother of pearl.

GLADYS. Forty one melody buttons! *(Moving closer to ABBOTT.)* Just waiting to be pressed!

ABBOTT. Look, ladies, I'm here on business.

GLADYS. Oh, Hazel, couldn't he?

AMERICA. Please?

GLADYS. Pretty please?

HAZEL. I suppose Grandpa wouldn't mind. Go ahead, Mr. Abbott—if you're gentleman enough! *(ABBOTT accepts the challenge. HAZEL nods to SWINDLES.)* Girls, strap him up!

(The SWINDLES help put the accordion on ABBOTT, occupying his attention while the rest of the LADIES huddle.)

GLADYS. He reminds me of Ramon Navarro.

RENNABELLE. He reminds me of Lon Chaney.

HAZEL. Well, there's something fishy about him, if you ask me. Mark my words, he's up to no good.

GLADYS. I think he's the bee's knees. *(The other ladies look at GLADYS as if she had lost her mind.)* He's everything the stars promised!

(ABBOTT, having the accordion in place, accidentally squeezes it as he is walking toward HAZEL and the others.)

HAZEL. Shh... here he comes... *(To ABBOTT.)* Go ahead, Mr. Abbott. Give the Dear Hearts a squeeze.

ABBOTT. It's been a long time. *(ABBOTT plays a wheezy cadence. Most of the LADIES, with the exception of HAZEL, applaud. ABBOTT relaxes.)* I was strictly amateur. Brass bands, mandolin orchestras... back home in Indianapolis.

RENNABELLE. Indianapolis?

GLADYS. Urbs nobilis!

AMERICA. *(Whistles.)* A city slicker!

HAZEL. *(Indifferently.)* I could see that by his shoes.

GLADYS. Do tell the Dear Hearts what it's like in the city, Mr. Abbott!

(RENNABELLE moves the microphone closer to ABBOTT, as the others, except HAZEL, gather around him.)

ABBOTT. *(Inspired.)* Oh, it's mighty exciting. *(MABEL & AZILEE begin soft underscoring: # 16 "Big City Theme")* Why, there's department stores, and picture shows, and miles and miles of cement sidewalks!

AMERICA. They got electric street cars where you come from?

ABBOTT. *(Proudly.)* Three of 'em!

RENNABELLE. Boy, would I love to ride an elevated train and go to the Follies!

GLADYS. City life must be grand. So much culture to absorb...

AMERICA. I went to a dog show in Fort Wayne once.

ABBOTT. Yeah, well, it's not all champagne and roses. Sometimes I just sit around—up in my penthouse of course—and the lonesomest feelings steal across my poor bosom. There's something deep down inside that I'm longing to say. Ah, but who's to care...

GLADYS. I do.

AMERICA. Sing us something!

ABBOTT. Right here, right now?

RENNABELLE. Nobody comes into Hazel Hunt's parlor without a song.

ABBOTT. Ladies, this is pure foolishness...

HAZEL. Foolishness? To sing? Why it's one of the most beautiful and eloquent things a human being is capable of.

GLADYS. *(Declaiming.)*

Pluck the Rose of Inspiration

Growing in the Field Above
Quench it with the Dew of Kindness
In the Vase of Truth and Love

ABBOTT. Emily Dickinson?

GLADYS. No... Gladys Fritts.

ABBOTT. *(Shouldering the accordion and stepping toward GLADYS, he thrusts out his chest and recites. GLADYS excitedly joins him on the last line.)*

Woodman spare that tree
Touch not a single bow
In youth it sheltered me
And I'll protect it now.

HAZEL. Great Scott, man. Get on with it. I'm running a radio station here, not a book shop.

ABBOTT. *(To GLADYS.)* Do you know "A Fireside A Pipe and A Pet" in E flat not too fast...

GLADYS. I love it. I love it.

ABBOTT. *(Pointing to the microphone.)* These things give me the shivers.

GLADYS. Mic fright. It happens to the best of us. *(She grabs a lampshade and puts it over the microphone.)* Just pretend it's a floor lamp. You'll be fine.

(During the course of the song, the LADIES are favorably impressed with ABBOTT's beautiful voice.)

 # 17: "A FIRESIDE, A PIPE & A PET"

ABBOTT.
I'VE KNOCKED AROUND
EVERY LITTLE TOWN
TRYING TO MAKE A DIME.
I'VE LIVED IN THE CITY
WHERE THE GALS ARE PRETTY;
I'VE HAD ME A MIGHTY GOOD TIME.

BUT NOW I'M OLDER
AND FEELING BOLDER,

SO I KNOW I'D REALLY BE SET
IF I HAD ME A PLACE,
SOME WIDE OPEN SPACE,
A FIRESIDE, A PIPE, AND A PET.

WITH A POUCH OF TOBACKY
AND A MUTT NAMED JACKY
SLEEPING AT MY FEET (WOOF),
A PICTURE OF MOTHER;
IS THERE ANY OTHER
WHOSE SMILE IS HALF AS SWEET?

(INSTRUMENTAL)

ABBOTT and GLADYS.
WITH A POUCH OF TOBACKY
AND A MUTT NAMED JACKY
SLEEPING AT MY FEET (WOOF),
A PICTURE OF MOTHER;
IS THERE ANY OTHER
WHOSE SMILE IS HALF AS SWEET?

LIFE WOULD BE THE BERRIES
IF MY DREAM CAME TRUE
    AMERICA, RENNABELLE & AZILEE.
IF HIS DREAM, HIS DREAM CAME TRUE
LIKE A GREAT BIG BOWL OF CHERRIES
WITH CREAM ENOUGH FOR TWO
GREAT BIG BOWL OF CREAM FOR TWO
    ABBOTT. (Solo.)
SO LOVE AND LAUGHTER'S
WHAT I'M AFTER
BUT I HAVEN'T FOUND IT YET,
AND IT WON'T BE COMPLETE
'TIL I'M THERE WITH MY SWEET,
A FIRESIDE, A PIPE, AND A PET;
A FIRESIDE, A PIPE AND A PET.

GLADYS. I hope all your dreams come true, Mr. Abbott.

ABBOTT. Why, thank you, Miss Fritts.

GLADYS. You can call me Gladys! *(Excitedly, to HAZEL.)* Did you observe his flatted third? Why, it's bold, it's incendiary. It's what Reverend Everhart called the blue note. **(To ABBOTT.)** Mr. Abbott, you're a born radio star.

HAZEL. Radio star, indeed! These days everybody wants to get into the act..

ABBOTT. Miss Hunt, if you're implying that I've come here to audition, you're sadly mistaken. I take my work very seriously.

GLADYS. *(Looking fondly at ABBOTT.)* I find his petulance irresistible! OH Hazel, couldn't we put him in the next number?

HAZEL. *(Sensing how uncomfortable ABBOTT is.)* Well, I don't see the harm. I've got a little time to fill. America, fetch me my duffel bag.

(AMERICA brings the bag to HAZEL.)

ABBOTT. *(Brandishing notes.)* But I'm on a case here. I can't be caterwaulin' away like an alley tom.

HAZEL. *(Yanking away ABBOTT's notes and handing him some sheet music which she has pulled from the bag.)* Now, now, Mr. Abbott. I'm sure Cedar Ridge would like to hear more of you. *(To microphone.)* Wouldn't you, Dear Hearts? *(To ABBOTT.)* But first, a little voice lesson. *(Patting his shoulders.)* Stand up straight! *(Poking his diaphragm.)* Suck in here! *(Poking his belly.)* Poochey out there. *(ABBOTT gasps.)* Now, bear down. *(ABBOTT grunts and his eyes bug out.)* Good! Just jump in after you've gotten the hang of a chorus or two!

RENNABELLE. *(Consulting watch.)* Hazel, we're right up on the hour.

HAZEL. *(Taking a pith helmet from the bag and setting it a little too firmly on ABBOTT's head.)* Let's give 'er the old college try. *(To GLADYS.)* Where are we traveling, Swami G?

(EVERYONE scrambles into pith helmets, etc., which are distributed from the duffel bag.)

GLADYS. The Belgian Congo! *(Drums begin.)* Picture, if you will, a path through the tangled tundra leading us to a secret lair hidden deep in the cool dark fern of the jungle.

AMERICA. Hark! Do you hear?

GLADYS. It's the distant drums of the Pygmy People.

HAZEL. Suddenly, from out of the gloom, like a shot, there is a burst of light..

#18: "EDNA JONES, THE ELEPHANT GIRL"

RENNABELLE. Is it a foxfire?

HAZEL. Is it a comet?

(HAZEL points out the lines to ABBOTT.)

ABBOTT. Is it Tarzan?

GLADYS. No!

ALL.
SWINGING THROUGH THE TREES IN B.V.D.'s
AMERICA and RENNABELLE.
WHO'S SHE?
ALL.
IT'S EDNA JONES
SHE'S THE ELEPHANT GIRL

LIVING IN THE TROPIC IS THE TOPIC
OF MISS EDNA JONES
SHE'S THE ELEPHANT GIRL
SHE GREW WEARY OF WASHING DISHES
PACKED HER BAGS, AND FOLLOWED HER FONDEST
      WISHES
NOW SHE'S GONNA BUNGLE IN THE DEEP, DARK
      JUNGLE
EDNA JONES, SHE'S THE ELEPHANT GIRL

(INSTRUMENTAL)

ABBOTT and GLADYS.
LIVING IN GRASS HUTS AND EATING NUTS TAKES GUTS
FOR EDNA JONES
   ALL.
SHE'S THE ELEPHANT GIRL.
   ABBOTT and GLADYS.
CARRYING A SPEAR, IT MIGHT SEEM QUEER,
   ALL.
BUT NOT FOR EDNA JONES
SHE'S THE ELEPHANT GIRL
SHE ALWAYS WANTED TO LIVE OFF THE LAND
AND BE THE LEADER OF A SWINGING DANCE BAND
A HERD OF GAZELLES
RINGING LITTLE BELLS
A BUNCH OF BABOONS
ON THE SLOWER TUNES
AN OLD ANTEATER
AND A COUPLE OF MOSQUITERS
TRADING OFF LICKS
WITH THE LITTLE DIK-DIKS
   GLADYS, AMERICA, ABBOTT, HAZEL.
EDNA JONES
   RENNABELLE, MABEL, AZILEE.
TO THE END, SHE'S A FRIEND OF THE ANIMALS
   GLADYS, AMERICA, ABBOTT, HAZEL.
EDNA JONES
   RENNABELLE, MABEL, AZILEE.
TO THE END, SHE'S A FRIEND OF THE ANIMALS

(INSTRUMENTAL.)

   ALL.
LATE AT NIGHT, YOU'LL FIND HER PEELING A BANANA
THINKING OF HER BOYFRIEND BACK IN TEXARKANA
HE'LL BE HANGING IN JUST LIKE GUNGA DIN
FOR EDNA JONES
   GLADYS, AMERICA, HAZEL, ABBOTT.
SHE'S THE ELEPHANT GIRL

RENNABELLE, MABEL, AZILEE.
THE STAR OF THE SHOW IS EDNA, YOU KNOW
    GLADYS, AMERICA, HAZEL, ABBOTT.
EDNA JONES
SHE'S THE ELEPHANT GIRL
    RENNABELLE, MABEL, AZILEE.
PLAYING THE FLUTE WHILE THE ELEPHANTS TOOT
    GLADYS, AMERICA, HAZEL, ABBOTT.
EDNA JONES
SHE'S THE ELEPHANT GIRL
    RENNABELLE, MABEL, AZILEE.
EV'RY NIGHT AT ELEVEN IT'S MUSIC MADE IN HEAVEN
    GLADYS, AMERICA, HAZEL, ABBOTT.
EDNA JONES
SHE'S THE ELEPHANT GIRL
    ALL.
SHE'S THE ELEPHANT GIRL.

(After the song, the telephone begins ringing, HAZEL answers it as
HAZELNUTS relax and pick up after the song.)

HAZEL. Hello, WGAL. *(Listens.)* Oh, hello Miss Peach. *(Listens.)* No we haven't all lost our minds! *(Listening, then to HAZELNUTS.)* Drat.! Miss Peach says she's getting interference from the Little Rock Amateur Hour. *(To microphone.)* Let's slide 'er all the way to the right, Dear Hearts. Everyone be sure and follow. One and a half full turns. *(HAZEL turns dial. ABBOTT, who has been flirting with GLADYS, begins to take an interest in what HAZEL is doing.)* This should knock us all the way to Tulsa. *(Into the telephone.)* How's that, Miss Peach?
HAZELNUTS. (Singing # 19A:)
TESTING, TESTING, ONE, TWO , THREE.

(ABBOTT is appalled.)

HAZEL. *(To HAZELNUTS.)* Clear as a bell!

(HAZEL hangs up the telephone.)

ABBOTT. *(To HAZEL.)* What in Sam Hill do you think you're doing?

HAZEL. I'll thank you not to talk that way in my parlor, Mr. Abbott.

ABBOTT. I'm not standing idly by while you make a mockery of broadcast codes.

HAZEL. I'll explain everything, if you'll just calm down. I'm forever getting interference from other stations, so I merely ease around the band until I find an empty space. Otherwise I'd never be heard.

ABBOTT. You can't change channels like they was ladies hats. That's wave jumping... Why, you're all air pirates. You're gypsies of the ether!

RENNABELLE. Gypsies!?

HAZELNUTS. (Singing # 19B:)
PLAY GYPSIES PLAY
MAKE THE MUSIC FAST...

ABBOTT. *(Abruptly cutting the HAZELNUTS off.)* Cedar Ridge is just another Shangri-La, and you... YOU... you're the Lotus Eaters!

GLADYS. You love Tennyson too?

(ABBOTT starts to take the license down from the wall.)

HAZEL. What in tarnation do you think you're doing?

ABBOTT. I'm revoking your license.

HAZEL. Unhand that document, young man! Why, the very idea. The ether is free. You can't put bars on the air!

ABBOTT. And you can't wander all over the broadcast band... you could be prosecuted.

AMERICA. You mean women's prison?

(MABEL gasps and swoons onto the piano keys. The other HAZEL-NUTS attend to her.)

HAZEL. How dare you threaten us!

ABBOTT. I'm afraid it's curtains for you ladies. I'm reporting you to the Department of Commerce.

(ABBOTT heads toward the telephone. GLADYS throws herself in front of it.)

GLADYS. How could you, Mr. Abbott?

ABBOTT. If you won't let me telephone I'll just go to the Western Union.

GLADYS. I beseech you, don't close the station down. You don't know what it means, to Hazel, to Cedar Ridge, to me.

ABBOTT. *(Pausing, then reaching for GLADYS' hand.)* Don't worry, pretty lady. *(GLADYS gives ABBOTT her hand. He kisses it.)* I'll see that you get time off for good behavior.

(ABBOTT grabs briefcase and walks out the front door.)

GLADYS. Mr. Abbott, I'm coming with you.

HAZEL. Gladys, what on earth?

GLADYS. Hazel, I've heard the call of the wild and I'm about to answer!

HAZEL. Gladys, you're not a flapper. You're a grown woman. You're vice president of the Sisters of Pythias.

GLADYS. *(Ripping off her Sisters of Pythias broach and throwing it on the floor—this action can be mimed—as the other HAZELNUTS gasp in horror.)* Not anymore. I've met my destiny. And his name is O.B. *(GLADYS rushes the door after ABBOTT.)* The stars don't lie!

(RENNABELLE and AMERICA rush to the window and watch GLADYS and ABBOTT.)

HAZEL. She's off her nut.

(Sound of motorcycle being cranked.)

AMERICA. He's cranking up his motor sickle.

RENNABELLE. Gladys is crawling on behind.

HAZEL. *(To SWINDLES.)* She'll ruin her stockings.

RENNABELLE. Too late now.

AMERICA. He's struggling, but she's got him in a death grip.

RENNABELLE. And they're off!

(Sound of motorcycle receding.)

HAZEL. Gladys would chase a moonbeam down a drainpipe.*
RENNABELLE. What are you going to do, Hazel?
HAZEL. We're still on the air. *(Realizing she has forgotten her radio audience, HAZEL advances to the microphone and says, sweetly.)* I certainly hope you're enjoying the program. *(RENNABELLE and AMERICA moan.)* Don't despair, Dear Hearts. I'll bring Gladys back. But don't touch that dial. I have a little story to tell you...

20: "PAGING THE ETHER/PLAY GYPSIES, PLAY"

HAZEL.
ON A LONELY BEACH IN PANAMA
A SHIPWRECKED CAPTAIN SAT
HUNGRY AND FAINT, WITH NO ONE TO HEAR HIS 'PLAINT
AS HE SWATTED OFF THE FLIES WITH HIS HAT

HE WAS THINKING OF HIS ONLY DAUGHTER
WOULD HE EVER SEE HER AGAIN
BACK IN BOSTON IT WAS CHRISTMAS—BUT HE'S
        STRANDED ON HIS ISTHMUS
WITH NOTHING BUT AN OLD TIN CAN

THEN HE HAPPENED ON A SMALL PIECE OF CRYSTAL
AND WOUND IT IN AN INCH OF ITS LIFE
WITH A LITTLE BIT OF CABLE THAT HE'D TAKEN FROM
        A GABLE
OF THE LIGHT HOUSE WHERE HE ONCE HAD A WIFE

SPARE HIM YOUR SYMPATHY, MY BRETHREN
TAKE HEED FROM HIS STORY AND BE STRONG
FOR OUR CAPTAIN HE WAS TIRELESS—OF THAT CAN HE
        MADE A WIRELESS
AND FROM FAR ACROSS THE FOAM HE HEARD A SONG:

*from Marcia M. Dodge

PAGING THE ETHER
SOUNDS ACROSS THE SKY
EACH TIME YOU HAVE A THOUGHT
I HAVE ONE TOO, THAT'S WHY
   with **RENNABELLE and AMERICA.**
YOU'RE NEVER ALONE
WHEN SOMEONE KNOWS YOUR HEART
   with **AZILEE.**
CLOSE COMMUNICATION
THOUGH WE'RE MANY MILES APART
   HAZEL and THE HAZELNUTS.
PAGING THE ETHER STRAIGHT UP TO THE STARS
MAYBE THEY CAN PICK US UP ON MERCURY AND MARS
   HAZEL.
THE WHISKERS OF A CAT
   RENNABELLE and AMERICA.
AND A LITTLE PIECE OF QUARTZ
   ALL.
YOU'LL BE HEARING MUSIC NOT TO MENTION NEWS
      AND SPORTS

DON'T YOU FRET, DEAR
   HAZEL.
JUST GO FISHING IN THE SKY
   ALL.
CAST A NET, DEAR
   HAZEL.
YOU COULD CATCH AN ANGEL
CROONING LIGHTLY
   ALL.
CALLING NIGHTLY
BEAMING THROUGH THE ETHER BRIGHTLY
   HAZEL. *(Spoken.)* Now!
   ALL.
PLAY GYPSIES PLAY
MAKE THE MUSIC FAST
PLAY GYPSIES PLAY
LET'S FORGET THE PAST

WHAT CARE WE FOR SORROW
WE'LL GO ROVING TOMORROW
SO STRIKE UP A TARANTELLA
AND PLAY GYPSIES PLAY

(TARANTELLA INSTRUMENTAL BREAK [VIOLIN])

STRIKE UP A TARANTELLA
AND PLAY GYPSIES...
    HAZEL. *(During the instrumental HAZEL has taken down the musket and is preparing to leave.)* Damn the torpedoes, full speed ahead. I'm coming, Gladys!

(HAZEL exits the front door as HAZELNUTS bravely continue.)

    HAZELNUTS.
ALWAYS BEEPING ALWAYS SENDING
NEVER SLEEPING NEVER ENDING
CLOSE COMMUNICATION
W—G—A—L
THOUGH WE'RE MANY MILES A—
    RENNABELLE.
PART
    as AMERICA and AZILEE sing.
LA LA LA LA LA LA LA LA LA
LA LA LA LA LA LA LA LA LA
    ALL.
SO PLAY GYPSIES PLAY

(The curtain falls.)

END OF ACT I

ACT II

*(The last movement of Berlioz' "The Damnation of Faust" is play-
ing as the curtain rises for Act II. The scene is the same. It is early
evening of the same day. The parlor is strewn with phonograph
records, newspapers, plates with half eaten cream cheese and olive sandwiches, etc. AMERICA is halfheartedly reading a maga-
zine. MISS AZILEE is wearily attempting to dust. MISS MABEL
is knitting. RENNABELLE is pretending she is conducting the
Berlioz, the sound of which is coming from the parlor phonograph.
She works herself into a frenzy as the music ends with a flourish.
We hear the sound of the phonograph needle scratching on the
record. RENNABELLE lifts up the needle.)*

RENNABELLE. We've been listening to "Pandemonium," from
The Damnation of Faust. This is Rennabelle Hatch. I'd like to welcome you back to the program. *(Picking up a book.)* Our classical
marathon continues with a reading of *PARADISE LOST.*

AMERICA. Can't we hear somethin' a little less tedious...

RENNABELLE. *(Aside to AMERICA.)* Look, I've already read
the funnies and the classified, twice. *(Putting the book down on the
table.)* Dear Hearts, I'd just like to say how very heavy are our hearts,
due to the desertion and disappearance of our own Masked Soprano,
Miss Gladys Fritts.

AMERICA. So, Miss Gladys, if you're out there listening, please
come back! It's a wild and wooly world. *(Aside, to RENNABELLE.)*
Thank God I'm just a fiddler.

RENNABELLE. As if that wasn't enough, late this afternoon
word came from the ball field that the Cedar Ridge Yellow Hammers
lost to the Brown Town Boll Weevils, 27 to 5, though our dear boys
did make a valiant effort out on the diamond, rallying in the bottom
of the ninth.

(MABEL sobs. She and AZILEE are taking the news badly.)

AMERICA. *(In an effort to soothe the SWINDLES and Cedar Ridge.)*
Oh somewhere in this favored land the sun is shining bright
The band is playing somewhere and somewhere hearts are bright
And somewhere men are laughing and little children shout
But there is no joy in Cedar Ridge—the Hammers have struck out!

(MABEL and AZILEE have taken no comfort from this.)

RENNABELLE. Friends, it seems as if our spirits could use a little reviving. America?

 # 21: "ROYAL RADIO"

AMERICA.
I GOT A HOME IN THE ROCK OF AGES
MY NAME'S WRITTEN IN THE BOOK OF PAGES
I GOT A KEY TO THE DOOR OF THE HEAVENLY HOME
I'LL BE WEARING THEM GOLDEN SLIPPERS
SNOW WHITE ROBES WITHOUT ANY ZIPPERS SINGING ON
THAT ROYAL RADIO
THERE'LL BE NO STATIC
THAT'S AUTOMATIC
NO TUBES OR WIRES
JUST HARPS AND LYRES
NO WHOOPS AND WHEEZES
JUST STUFF THAT PLEASES
BROADCASTING A JOYFUL NOISE AROUND

with AZILEE.
I'M GONNA SING WITH THE ANGEL BAND
RIDE ALL AROUND THE PROMISED LAND
PLAYING IN THOSE PALACES OF GOLD
NO MORE SORROW, NO MORE BLUES
I'M GONNA SPREAD THE HEAVENLY NEWS
SINGING ON THAT ROYAL RADIO

(INSTRUMENTAL.)

with RENNABELLE, MABEL and AZILEE.
WHEN THE ROAD GETS ROUGH AND BUMPY
WHEN THE GRAVY'S COLD AND LUMPY
AND MISFORTUNE TRIES TO LAY YOU LOW
DON'T GIVE UP YOU BEST INTENTION
'TIL YOU'VE TRIED THAT NEW INVENTION
THAT THEY CALL THE ROYAL RADIO

NO TROUBLE OR TRIAL
ON THE HEAVENLY DIAL
NO SIN, NO SORROW
IN THAT TOMORROW
NO INTERFERENCE
    AMERICA. (Solo.)
WITH PERSEVERANCE
YOU CAN SEND A SIGNAL ROUND THE WORLD.
    with RENNABELLE and AZILEE.
LISTEN TO THAT EXALTATION
TUNING IN TO THE HOLY STATION
ON THE CHANNEL OF THE SANCTIFIED.
WE'LL TAKE OFF IN A CLOUD OF GLORY,
TELLIN' THAT FAMILIAR STORY
EV'RY DAY ON THE ROYAL RADIO.
    AMERICA. (Solo.)
WE'LL TAKE OFF IN A CLOUD OF GLORY,
TELLIN' THAT FAMILIAR STORY
EV'RY DAY ON THE ROYAL RADI—
    ALL.
O.
    RENNABELLE. Well, that certainly lightened my load, America. Did I tell you about Hazel's new coffee trick? Just stir a dash of All-spice, and a jigger of Horehound Compound, into your afternoon cup. Gives it such a festive, exotic flavor. And boy, could we use some.

(RENNABELLE offers the cup to AMERICA. AMERICA tastes it and makes a face, spitting it out.)

AMERICA. You put in too much Allspice.

RENNABELLE. *(Vexed.)* Next time you can mix it up.

(The telephone rings.)

AMERICA. I'll get it. *(Both girls dive for it. AMERICA gets there first and sticks her tongue out at RENNABELLE.)* Hello. WGAL. *(To the other HAZELNUTS.)* It's the Mayor! *(Listening.)* Oh, sweet of you to offer, sir, but everything's under control. What's that? *(To the other HAZELNUTS.)* Oh dear, he says our signal's getting weak.

RENNABELLE. I've been waiting to do this!

(RENNABELLE puts on the headphones and starts turning the transmitter dial.)

AMERICA. Rennabelle, we're not supposed to touch that thing.

RENNABELLE. This is an emergency. I'm turning her back to the left, Dear Hearts, so everyone be sure and follow... all the way to 460.

AMERICA. But we've never ever been there before...

RENNABELLE. That's right, America. Where angels fear to tread. *(RENNABELLE turns the dial.)* How's this, Dear Hearts?

(RENNABELLE signals to the other HAZELNUTS.)

HAZELNUTS. (Singing # 22.)
TESTING, TESTING, ONE, TWO , THREE.

AMERICA. *(Listening, then reporting to the others.)* Clearer and stronger than ever!

RENNABELLE. I knew it would work! Now if Hazel would just let me be in charge of it all the time.

AMERICA. *(Into telephone.)* No kiddin? The whole town? The Baptists? The Methodists? How do you like that! Um hum... What's that?... I'll see to it at once. You take care now.

(AMERICA hangs up.)

RENNABELLE. *(Impatiently.)* What'd he say, what'd he say?

AMERICA. The whole town's in an uproar. The churches are getting hot. They're saying the Almighty doesn't abide by wavelength codes, so why should Hazel Hunt!

RENNABELLE. Dear Hearts! *(To AMERICA.)* Anything else?

AMERICA. He needs two more bottles of horehound

RENNABELLE. Gee, things are really heatin' up.

AMERICA. *(Concerned.)* Maybe you'd better check the barometer.

RENNABELLE. Say, there's an idea...

#23: "THE WEATHER SONG"

ALL.
IT COULD RAIN,
IT COULD SNOW,
IT COULD CLEAR,
IT COULD BLOW.
HOW YOU GONNA KNOW?
HOW YOU GONNA TELL?
RENNABELLE.
JUST STAY TUNED TO G–A–L.
ALL.
FAIR OR FOUL? WHO KNOWS WHETHER?
RENNABELLE.
JUST ASK RENNABELLE FOR THE WEATHER.

RENNABELLE. Hi, Cedar Ridge!! Get out your canoes and banjos 'cause it's going to be a lovely evening! *(Sound of a thunder clap.)* With a slight chance of rain.

AMERICA, AZILEE, MABEL.
LOTS OF TIMES SHE GETS IT WRONG,
RENNABELLE.
BUT I LOVE TO SING THIS SONG.

(INSTRUMENTAL TAG.)

(At the end of the song we hear severe static from out of the transmitter, and then the sound of some phrases being spoken by a French radio announcer.)

VOICE OF FRENCH RADIO ANNOUNCER. Bon Soir, mesdames et messieurs. Je suis Jean Louis Casanova, pour Radio Montreal. Et maintenant, une chanson du Maurice Chevalier.

(There follows a first line or two from a period Maurice Chevalier song.)

AMERICA. Holy cats! We been invaded.

RENNABELLE. America, don't be a duck. *(RENNABELLE rushes over to the transmitter.)* I'll just twist a few knobs here. *(RENNABELLE jiggles the dials. We hear more static.)* I'll give her an extra tug, just in case.

(The transmitter knob comes off in her hand, then the static stops.)

AMERICA. Now look what you've done.

RENNABELLE. Hello, hello out there. This is WGAL in Cedar Ridge. Dear Hearts, are we coming through? Ring me up on the Royal Telephone and tell me if we are. That's Katydid 23... *(RENNABELLE pauses, then says, anxiously.)* And I certainly hope you're enjoying the program.

AMERICA. What are you gonna do now, Miss Smarty-Pants?

RENNABELLE. *(Picking up the book, turning to the first page and frantically beginning to read:)*
Of Man's first disobedience, and the fruit
Of that forbidden tree whose mortal taste
Brought death into the world and all our woe...

(MABEL and AZILEE, having each donned tiaras (a la Ma Rainey), decide to take matters in their own hands and entertain. They interrupt RENNABELLE's reading with the vamp to "Buster".)

 # 24 "BUSTER, HE'S A HOT DOG NOW"

MABEL and AZILEE.
BUSTER WAS A RUNT,
COULDN'T EVEN HUNT
WITH THE BIG DOGS WHEN THEY'D RUN.
HE'D JUST STAY AT HOME

WITH HIS LITTLE BONE.
BUSTER NEVER HAD MUCH FUN.

'TIL ONE DAY HE MET A
PACK OF WILD CHIHUAHUAS,
GOT INTO SOME CHILI
MADE BY MEXICAN MAMAS.
NOW HE'S A HIGH STEPPER
SINCE HE'S HAD HIS PEPPER.
BUSTER, HE'S A HOT DOG NOW.

BUSTER TOOK A TRIP
ON A LITTLE SHIP,
ENDED UP IN GAY PAREE
HE WENT ON A SPREE
IN THE TUILLIERIE
HE MET A POODLE NAMED FIFI.
SHE PUT HIM IN A HACK AND
TOOK HIM TO THE FOLLIES
WHERE SHE DID THE CAN-CAN
WITH A LINE OF COLLIES.
SINCE THAT PRETTY POODLE
COOKED HIS LITTLE NOODLE,
BUSTER, HE'S A HOT DOG NOW.

(INSTRUMENTAL and MISS MABEL's DANCE BREAK.)

'TIL ONE DAY HE MET A
PACK OF WILD CHIHUAHUAS,
GOT INTO SOME CHILI
MADE BY MEXICAN MAMAS.
NOW HE'S A HIGH STEPPER
SINCE HE'S HAD HIS PEPPER.
BUSTER, HE'S A HOT DOG NOW.

*(After the song, GLADYS comes in the front door, followed by
    ABBOTT, with his arms raised, followed by HAZEL who is train-
    ing the musket on ABBOTT.)*

RENNABELLE. Holy cats! You found 'em!

AMERICA. I've never been so glad to see anyone in my life!

RENNABELLE. Where have you been?

GLADYS. *(Disappointedly.)* Nowhere. We never left the country. HE got lost.

ABBOTT. SHE spilt a bottle of violet water all over my road map. Bleached out the entire Midwest.

HAZEL. Found 'em parked by the Nimrod River Dam.

RENNABELLE and AMERICA. Parked?

ABBOTT. I was out of gas.

GLADYS. HE couldn't get it started.

ABBOTT. Well if I could've I would've so's I could dump Sarah Bernhardt here.

GLADYS. You're no Valentino.

ABBOTT. You're no Vilma Banky.

HAZEL. Friends, friends...

GLADYS. Oh, Hazel, he's nothing like I thought. He doesn't give a fig about the things I adore: Emerson, Wordsworth, Longfellow. *(HAZEL directs GLADYS to the microphone. GLADYS, over the course of reciting the following verse, is overcome with self pitying emotion.)*

By the shores of Gitche Gumee
By the shining Big-Sea-Water
Stood the wigwam of Nokomis,
Daughter of the Moon, Nokomis.
Dark behind it rose the forest,
Rose the black and gloomy pine-trees
Rose the firs with cones upon them;
Bright before it beat the water
Beat the clear and sunny water
Beat the shining Big-Sea-Water

(GLADYS collapses.)

HAZEL. I've never seen her like this before. *(She pauses, then reconsiders.)* Well... hardly ever. *(She pokes the musket at ABBOTT.)* You've got to do something.

ABBOTT. Me? What?

AMERICA. How about a ballad?

RENNABELLE. We are on the air.

HAZEL. *(Recalling herself to the radio audience, she advances to the microphone and says sweetly.)* I certainly hope you're enjoying the program. *(Urgently, to RENNABELLE.)* Rennabelle, some sheet music.

RENNABELLE. *(Grabbing a song off the top of the pile and handing it to ABBOTT.)* Here, Mr. Abbott. The song plugger down at the furniture store's been pushing this one.

ABBOTT. *(Reading.)* "Why Did You Make Me Love You?"

(GLADYS sobs mournfully.)

ABBOTT. "As popularized by Miss Pansy Spry of Pomona, New York." But it's got four flats.

HAZEL. *(Aiming musket at ABBOTT.)* It's like I used to tell my students... Just take a deep breath and pretend this is Carnegie Hall!

25: "WHY DID YOU MAKE ME LOVE YOU?"

ABBOTT.
I WAS CONTENT TO DRIFT ALONG
THE GENTLY ROLLING STREAM
I HAD MY DAYS
MY CAREFREE WAYS
MEANT ALL THE WORLD TO ME.
THEN YOU APPEARED
AND, AS I FEARED
LIFE CAUGHT UP WITH ME
AND SO THAT'S WHY
I'D LIKE TO TRY
AND SOLVE THIS MYSTERY

WHY DID YOU MAKE ME LOVE YOU?
WHY DID YOU MAKE ME STAY
YOU LOCKED ME UP LIKE A NAUGHTY PUP
AND THREW THE KEY AWAY

SURE AS THE STARS ABOVE ME
STICK IN THE MILKY WAY
I'M UP IN THE BLUE
WHAT CAN I DO?
OH, WHY DID YOU MAKE ME LOVE YOU?

(INSTRUMENTAL.)

GLADYS. *(Over instrumental.)* Don't anyone mind about me. I'll just go up to the widow's walk and ponder my life as it moves into the evening shadows. I'll scan the horizon for my Odysseus. Maybe he'll still come—he doesn't have to be a tenor.

(GLADYS starts to head for the door, but HAZEL taps her on the shoulder.)

HAZEL. Gladys... may I have this dance?

(HAZEL, still holding the musket, waltzes with GLADYS as ABBOTT finishes the song.)

ABBOTT.
SURE AS THE STARS ABOVE ME
STICK IN THE MILKY WAY
I'M UP IN THE BLUE
WHAT CAN I DO?
OH, WHY DID YOU MAKE ME LOVE YOU?

(The LADIES have all been deeply moved by the song and ABBOTT's performance.)

AMERICA. Anybody who sings that good can't be all bad.
HAZEL. *(Putting down the musket.)* I hate to admit it, Mr. Abbott, but that was lovely. Rarely, in all my years of teaching music, have I heard such pure dulcet tones. *(Indicating accordion.)* You've got a nice touch too. *(Shaking her head.)* What a waste.
ABBOTT. Waste? Waste of what?
HAZEL. God given talent, that's all. Go ahead. Be a Hoover pup:

slink down the back alleys of power, obeying the big man's bidding.

ABBOTT. I have a job to do.

HAZEL. But don't' you see? You've got what it takes.

ABBOTT. Look, I appreciate your encouragement. You're a regular bunch, but this is official business here. There's policy to consider. There's standards to maintain.

GLADYS. *(Falling to her knees before ABBOTT.)* Mr. Abbott. I implore you. Think about what you're doing. To you, WGAL is just wires and tubes and codes. But to us, it's a mighty voice, our very spirit, as wild and free as the ether itself. To silence it would be unbearably cruel. I for one should never forgive you.

ABBOTT. *(Pausing, then picking up his briefcase and saying, resolutely.)* Sorry, but I've got to see a man about a dog.

(ABBOTT starts to walk away.)

GLADYS. *(Grabbing hold of ABBOTT.)* Stay, stay, but a little while.

HAZEL. For heaven's sake! Gladys, get up. Let the poor man go. He's got his "career" to consider. *(Sweetly to ABBOTT.)* Oh, Mr. Abbott, just one kind favor—if you would?

ABBOTT. *(With irritation.)* What's that?

HAZEL. Join us on one last number. For old time's sake.

ABBOTT. *(Impatiently.)* Okay, but make it snappy. I got to cable my district superintendent right away.

HAZEL. You know, you remind me of my Grandpa Hunt more and more every minute.

ABBOTT. How's that?

HAZEL. *(Pointing to Grandpa Hunt's portrait on the wall.)* Grandpa Hunt was a died in the wool Republican too. He'd get fired up about the queerest things. For instance, he couldn't abide pets in the house. Now Grandma Hunt she was a Democrat. And she had the cutest little Siamese named Tina. One cold dark night Grandpa Hunt wouldn't let Tina in the parlor. "How would you feel," Grandma asked him, "if you had to stay outside in the dead of Winter?" And to prove her point she locked Grandpa in the toolshed and wrote this song... And it's been a Democratic favorite ever since. Swami G?

GLADYS. Bundle up Cedar Ridge, we're journeying to the frigid peaks of Siberia.

(HAZEL seats ABBOTT in a chair and gives him the sheet music for "Kittens In The Snow".)

 # 26: "KITTENS IN THE SNOW"

GLADYS, RENNABELLE and AMERICA.
WE'RE KITTENS IN THE SNOW
WE'VE GOT NO PLACE TO GO
WE CAME OUTSIDE TO PLAY
AND LOST OUR LITTLE WAY
OH, WON'T YOU HELP US, PLEASE
BEFORE OUR WHISKERS FREEZE
WE'RE ON OUR KITTY KNEES
with ABBOTT and HAZEL.
MEOW MEOW MEOW MEOW
MEOW MEOW MEOW MEOW MEOW
WE'RE IN DISTRESS
OUR S.O.S. IS
MEOW MEOW MEOW
GLADYS, RENNABELLE and AMERICA.
SUDDENLY WE SAW A GREAT BIG BEAR
WITHOUT ANY HAIR
IT WAS THE ABOMINABLE SNOWMAN
HE SAID
ABBOTT.
BOO
I'LL TELL YOU WHAT I'LL DO
I'LL MAKE A KITTEN STEW

(ABBOTT roars.)

GLADYS, RENNABELLE and AMERICA.
OOOHHH
WE'RE JUST QUIVERING SHIVERING KITTENS
WITHOUT BOOTS AND WITHOUT MITTENS
OOOHHH

(INSTRUMENTAL)

GLADYS, RENNABELLE and AMERICA.
WE'RE KITTENS IN THE SNOW
THE HOUR IS GETTING LATE
THE BEAST IS FOLDING NAPKINS
HE'S SET ANOTHER PLATE
FOR MR. FRANKENSTEIN
THEY'RE TALKING ABOUT WINE
AND WONDERING WHAT KIND
GOES WITH
   with HAZEL and ABBOTT.
MEOW MEOW MEOW MEOW
MEOW MEOW MEOW MEOW MEOW
WE'RE IN DISTRESS
OUR S.O.S. IS
MEOW MEOW MEOW.
   GLADYS, RENNABELLE and AMERICA.
SUDDENLY WE SAW A ST. BERNARD
RUN INTO THE YARD
WITH SEVERAL TROOPS OF CANADIAN MOUNTIES
FOLLOWED BY THE CZAR
IN HIS ROYAL CAR
SMOKING A CIGAR—HA HA HA
THEY CAUGHT THAT AWFUL BEAST
AND SENT HIM TO THE EAST
WHERE HE WAS REHABILITATED BY A KINDLY PRIEST
AND NOW HE DRIVES A BUS
IT'S ALL BECAUSE OF US
   with HAZEL and ABBOTT.
WE'RE KITTENS IN THE NEWS
HO HO
WE KNOW
IT'S SO
THERE'S PLACES WE CAN GO
AND WE'RE IN ALL THE MAGAZINES EATING SARDINES
THE FAMOUS KITTENS IN THE SNOW

(Having diverted ABBOTT through the actions of the song, HAZEL
and GLADYS have managed, by the end, to tie him to the chair,

using yarn, or clothesline, or scarves, etc.)

ABBOTT. *(Struggling against his restraints.)* Let me go, let me go this instant! Czars, cats, Frankenstein. I had a feeling you was Reds. Release me at once!

GLADYS. *(Giggling.)* Not till you promise to be a good little inspector!

ABBOTT. I'll show you—

HAZEL. *(Stuffing a half eaten sandwich into his mouth.)* How's the cream cheese and olives?

(The telephone rings.)

AMERICA. I'll get it.

(AMERICA answers the telephone. At the same time we hear a "thunk" as a mailbag is tossed onto the porch.)

RENNABELLE. *(Going out to get the mail bag.)* Thanks Gus!

AMERICA. It's Mr. Hitchcock. Petunia just had thirteen little piglets!

HAZEL. I guess pork futures are looking pretty good.

RENNABELLE. *(Bringing in a large bag of mail.)* Special delivery! It's all wires and telegrams and things.

HAZEL. I've never seen so much mail! *(To SWINDLES.)* Girls?

(The SWINDLES begin # 27: "Mail Bag Rag Reprise." The LADIES begin opening envelopes and reading the messages. ABBOTT is chewing the sandwich and intently studying the SWINDLES. HAZEL notices him.)

HAZEL. Aren't they wonderful, Mr. Abbott.

(ABBOTT mutters with the sandwich in his mouth.)

GLADYS. *(Reading telegram.)* Here's one from a Mr. Rudolf Friml. "Dear WGAL. I especially appreciate the vocal renderings of your splendid soprano, Miss Gladys Fritts!" Je suis enchantee, I'm sure.

HAZEL. *(Opening an envelope and reading the message inside.)* Here's one from Kalamazoo! "Dear WGAL. You have the best live drama around. I'd love to listen to you all day long, but I've got to go. The Showboat's coming! Sincerely, Miss Edna Ferber."

AMERICA. Little ole WGAL... who'd've thunk it!

RENNABELLE. Would you listen to this—it's from Nova Scotia: "Dear WGAL, we just picked up your station on the British American band. *(ABBOTT manages to maneuver himself to see the transmitter dial.)* We're intrigued by your Horehound Compound. We'd like to order two dozen bottles. Cordially yours, the MacKensies of Gander."

(ABBOTT chewing and muttering more excitedly.)

HAZEL. *(Looking quizzically at RENNABELLE and AMERICA.)* I wonder how we got so far away?

AMERICA. I guess it's that clean, clear Arkansas air.

GLADYS. It's Divine Will!

ABBOTT. *(Having chewed up and swallowed the sandwich.)* It's the Canadian Government channel, that's what it is.

HAZEL. *(Sternly.)* Girls, what have you done?

RENNABELLE. We couldn't help it, Hazel. You were gone, and the knob just came off in my hand.

ABBOTT. *(Apoplectic.)* My case is complete! So, you thought you'd pulled the wool over my eyes, ladies? Well, I didn't just fall off the turnip truck. No siree, not O.B. Abbott!

HAZEL. What are you going to do about it?

ABBOTT. *(Maneuvering his chair to the musket.)* Get loose from Harpies and go down to the Western Union. *(Maneuvering the musket between his legs.)* And kindly don't attempt to impede me. *(With his feet, he raises the barrel toward the ladies.)* I'm armed.

HAZEL. *(Pointing to the musket.)* That old thing? Full of cobwebs. Couldn't kill a fly.

ABBOTT. You mean...

HAZEL. Better stick around, son. There's chicken and dumplings for supper.

RENNABELLE. *(Reading more telegrams.)* Here's a wire from Smiling Billy Cathay and his California Movieland Syncopators?

AMERICA. Smiling Billy!

GLADYS. I just love his music!

RENNABELLE. He wants go give Miss Mabel and Miss Azilee and featured spot on the Orpheum Vaudeville Circuit.

HAZEL. Just think of that, girls!

AMERICA. I can see it now: "The Swindle Sisters"—up there in e-lectric lights.

ABBOTT. Hold the fort... Did you say Swindle Sisters? *(Staring at the SWINDLES.)* That moniker... those familiar smirks. And that "music" you ladies were playing.

*(SWINDLES obligingly resume at **measure 11 of # 27: "Mail Bag Rag Reprise".**)*

HAZEL. *(Proudly.)* It's the Mail Bag Rag!

ABBOTT. Mail bag rag, my eye. THAT was the "Tennessee Tickle".

(The SWINDLES stop playing.)

ABBOTT. Holy Kannapolis! If it'd been a snake it would've bit me... Miss Hunt, something vile has crawled into your parlor!

HAZEL. Merciful heavens! What?

ABBOTT. Anarchy! It's all coming back to me now: Haymarket Square, a dark November day, and angry mob. Senator Lodge was trying to make a speech. All of a sudden the handbags started flying. A slew of suffering suffragettes stormed the soapbox. They tied up the Senator with reapers' rope.

(ABBOTT stares, in horror, at the ropes and/or yarn binding him to the chair.)

AMERICA. *(To HAZEL.)* I thought you said it was clothesline.

(HAZEL shushes AMERICA.)

ABBOTT. Oh how they taunted that venerable old gent. They stuck matches in the soles of his Oxfords and lit 'em. Then they shredded his top hat with pinking shears, and tossed it in the lily pond, right before his very eyes. *(To SWINDLES.)* I knew your mugs were familiar. These are the famous Blue Stockings.

RENNABELLE and AMERICA. Famous?

ABBOTT. These old dames are suspected of sedition in sixteen states.

(MABEL and AZILEE brandish pinking shears toward ABBOTT.)

HAZEL. Mr. Abbott, you must consider Miss Mabel and Miss Azilee's feelings. That's all behind them now. They're model citizens, pillars of the community. I was proud to give them refuge. It was the Pythian thing to do.

28: "OLD GALS"

HAZEL, AZILEE and MABEL.
OLD GALS ARE THE BEST PALS AFTER ALL
WHAT GOOD TIMES WE HAVE TO RECALL
LIKE FINE WINE AND CEDAR
SOME THINGS JUST GROW SWEETER AS TIME GOES BY

HAZEL.
OLD FRIENDS ARE THE BEST FRIENDS
YES IT'S TRUE
AZILEE and MABEL.
WE ALWAYS SEEM TO UNDERSTAND YOU
HAZEL, AZILEE and MABEL.
THO' LIFE THROWS US PUNCHES
WE'LL KEEP FIXING LUNCHES
TILL TIME GOES BY

HAZEL. *(Turning MABEL and AZILEE's faces toward ABBOTT.)* Be truthful, son. Are these the faces of Anarchy?

ABBOTT. *(To HAZEL.)* We'll let the Department of Commerce decide. I'm sorry, sister, but you're in deep dirt. First the wave jumping, then the moonshining, and now this... this... *(ABBOTT makes a gesture with his head that includes the whole parlor.)* conspiracy!

You realize of course Mr. Hoover will order a grand investigation. Your station will be sealed; your operation suspended; and, your frequency assigned to a network.

HAZEL. Network? Well I say curses to your Mr. Hoover. I'll go to Washington and chain myself to the columns of the Department of Commerce, if that's what it takes! I'll talk to ole Rubber Face himself. Then I'll dance on his desk!

ABBOTT. How dare you speak that way about a man who may someday be the President of the United States. Besides, Mr. Hoover's a very busy official. He's got more important things to do than concern himself about a station of mere amateur status. That's MY job... soon as I get untied.

GLADYS. Amateur?

HAZEL. More important thing? Like what? Building some silly old dam? Well, the next time you see your Mister Hoover, you can tell him something for me.

ABBOTT. What's that?

HAZEL. You can tell him Hazel Hunt said:

#29: "A GAL'S GOT TO DO WHAT A GAL'S GOT TO DO"

HAZEL.
A GAL'S GOT TO DO WHAT A GAL'S GOT TO DO.
SHE'S GOT TO BE TRUE TO HER FRIENDS.
SHE'D BE AS OLD AS METHUSELAH
IF SHE WAITED AROUND FOR YOU MEN.
SHE HAS TO MANAGE SOMEHOW SOME WAY
IF SHE'S GOING TO TAKE CARE OF HER BROOD.
LIKE A MAMA LION, SHE'LL GO ON TRYIN',
AND THAT'S WHAT A GAL'S GOT TO DO.

A GAL'S GOT TO DO WHAT A GAL'S GOT TO DO.
THERE'S THINGS THAT SHE OUGHT TO KNOW,
LIKE WHEN TO SPEAK OUT AND WHEN TO BE QUIET,
ESPECIALLY ON RADIO.
SHE OUGHT TO BE PATIENT, FORGIVING, AND SWEET,
AND IT PAYS TO BE HUMBLE, TOO.
SINCE ADAM AND EVE, SHE'S BEEN TAUGHT TO BELIEVE

THAT THAT'S WHAT A GAL'S GOT TO DO.

THINK OF THE SHUT-IN WHOSE ONLY JOY
IS A FRIEND AT THE END OF THE DIAL.
AND THE PRISONER IN THE COUNTY JAI,
THE RADIO BRINGS HIM A SMILE.
AND THE LONELY HOUSEWIFE, HOW WOULD SHE FEEL
IF OUR SIGNAL DIDN'T COME THROUGH?
SHE'D STAY IN BED WITH A RAG ON HER HEAD.
IS THAT ALL A GAL'S GOT TO DO?

SO LET IT RING FORM THE TOP OF THE MOUNTAIN
FROM THE TIP OF THE STEEPLES AND SPIRES
THE AIRWAVES ARE FREE; THEY'RE NOT MEANT TO BE
THE PAWN OF POLITICAL LIARS
SOMEONE'S GOT TO TELL IT, I'M GOING TO SPELL IT.
FOR THE NATION FOR ME AND FOR YOU
SO APPLY IT WITH GRACE, PUT SOME ROUGE ON YOUR
        FACE
CAUSE THAT'S WHAT A GAL'S GOT TO DO
THAT'S WHAT A GAL'S GOT TO DO.

HAZEL. *(Loosening ABBOTT's ropes.)* So go ahead, Mr. Abbott. Sic the hounds on us if you must. Just remember this: the only real amateur in this parlor is you. In the meantime, we have a radio station to save. Come on, girls.

(HAZEL and the rest of the LADIES proudly file past ABBOTT and resume various duties: reading mail, checking transmitter, straightening up the sheet music, etc.)

ABBOTT. *(Removing the ropes, rubbing his wrists and muttering to the LADIES as they pass.)* Bushwhacked by a bunch of poetry spoutin' channel jumpers! Luring me into their cozy little den, trying to turn me into a sissified sap full of hair tonic...

(The telephone rings.)

HAZEL. *(Answering.)* Hello, WGAL

ABBOTT. *(Angrily, to GLADYS in particular.)* Canoodle-ing with my affections.

HAZEL. *(To the HAZELNUTS.)* It's long distance from New York City!

HAZELNUTS. New York City?

(HAZELNUTS crowd around HAZEL. ABBOTT is also interested in the telephone call.)

HAZEL. *(To HAZELNUTS.)* It's a Mr. Sarnoff. Claims he's the President of the National Broadcasting Company.

ABBOTT. Sarnoff? Say it isn't so.

HAZEL. It seems our signal's been interrupting their national network.

ABBOTT. There's still time. I'll cable Mr. Hoover. I'll explain everything.

HAZEL. Mr. Sarnoff says they're airing a trans-America radio broadcast... from the Grand Ballroom of the Waldorf Astoria!

AMERICA. Just think of it. Waldorf Salad—tubs of it!

ABBOTT. *(To the LADIES.)* Justice will be served. You ladies'll be wearing stripes and crushing rocks till doomsday.

HAZEL. What's that, Mr. Sarnoff?

ABBOTT. Say, I might even get a promotion for this!

HAZEL. You'd love to have the Hazelnuts do a few musical selections to close the broadcast?

ABBOTT. *(With hand on doorknob, opening it to leave.)* I'm off to Washington—and don't try to stop me!

HAZEL. You're particularly impressed with our tenor, Mr. O.B. Abbott?

ABBOTT. *(Closing the door and taking off his hat.)* I never really liked government work anyway. Ladies, my investigation is officially canceled.

(ABBOTT drops his briefcase. The LADIES rejoice.)

HAZEL. *(Into telephone.)* Yes sir, Mr. Sarnoff! We'll be ready! *(She puts the receiver down, off the hook and says to the HAZEL-NUTS:)* Gird your loins, girls. We go on the air at 8 o'clock.

RENNABELLE. *(Consulting her watch.)* We only have a few minutes!

AMERICA. What are we going to sing?

GLADYS. We'll have to do "The Wedding of the Flowers." *(To ABBOTT.)* I'm the bride. Perhaps you'd like to be the groom?

RENNABELLE. Miss Mabel gets so weary of it.

ABBOTT. Swell!

HAZEL. Don't forget "Whispering Pines." It was Grandpa Hunt's favorite.

ABBOTT. "Whispering Pines?" I love that song.

HAZEL. You do? Dear boy! *(To HAZELNUTS.)* That does it, girls. What do you say we induct him!

ABBOTT. Induct him?

RENNABELLE. Why it's cream in the can!

AMERICA. With that silvery voice...

HAZEL. Those pear shaped tones...

GLADYS. And the biggest Sword of Apollo I've ever seen!

ABBOTT. You mean...

HAZEL. That's right, son. You have all the makings of a nut—a Hazelnut, that is!

ABBOTT. Me, a Hazelnut!

30 "INDUCTION"

(During the Induction music, the LADIES ceremoniously pass a ukulele, on to another, until it ends in ABBOTT's hands. ABBOTT holds it up and gazes at it as if it were the Holy Grail.)

HAZEL. *(As music concludes.)* Congratulations, Mr. Abbott. You're a real filbert now.

ABBOTT. Thank you, Miss Hunt!

HAZEL. You can call me Hazel. By the way, what does the "O.B." stand for?

ABBOTT. *(Confidentially.)* It's a long story.

RENNABELLE. *(Consulting her watch.)* Everybody hurry up—there's not a second to lose.

HAZEL. *(Pointing to the transmitter.)* O.B. you do the honors.

(The LADIES rush about, getting props, and preparing for the broadcast: doing vocal warm ups, tuning, primping, etc. ABBOTT has put on headphones to monitor the proceedings.)

ABBOTT. Quiet in the studio!

(We hear the voice of an NBC RADIO ANNOUNCER coming through the speaker horn.)

NBC ANNOUNCER. "... heard all across America. And now, Ladies and Gentlemen, for a very special treat we take you, via telephonic hook-up, to the foothills of the Ozarks, where the crystal waters flow and the Razorbacks rule. Come in, Radio Gals!"

(ABBOTT excitedly points to HAZEL, and nods, giving her the green light.)

HAZEL. *(Loudly, into micropone.)* Hello, everybody! I'm Hazel Hunt and this is:
HAZELNUTS. (Singing # 31: "Station I.D. # 2.)
WGAL
IN CEDAR RIDGE
ARKANSAS
HAZEL. Brought to you by...

 # 32: "HOREHOUND #3"

GLADYS, RENNABELLE, AZILEE, AMERICA, ABBOTT and MABEL.
HOREHOUND COMPOUND
NOW IT'S BEEN IMPROVED.
ONCE YOU HAVE TRIED IT
YOU WILL BE MOVED.
SIS CURLS HER HAIR WITH IT,
DAD SOAKS HIS DENTURES IN IT,
MOM CLEANS THE FLOOR WITH IT,
JUNIOR HAS ADVENTURES IN IT.
HOREHOUND COMPOUND, IT'S THE STUFF.

HAZEL. From a secret recipe handed down by Grandpa Hunt. I can still see him, up at Lake Kitchykoo, with his squeeze box, his Bible, and a can of worms. "Come along, children," his dear old voice echoes through the halls of Time. "Let's leave this suffering world behind, and go fish!"

#33: "WHISPERING PINES"

ALL.
THERE'S A PLACE I DREAM OF
BY A GREEN SHORELINE
THERE I LONG TO WANDER,
'NEATH THE WHISPERING PINES.
ECHOES OF THE RUDE WORLD
VANISH INTO SPACE.
PEACEFULNESS ENFOLDS ME
IN THAT HAPPY PLACE.

FONDLY I REMEMBER
SWINGING ON THOSE VINES
CAREFREE DAYS OF SUMMER
'NEATH THE WHISPERING PINES

SITTING BY THE FIRESIDE,
DREAMING OF THAT PLACE
BRINGS A SMILE OF GLADNESS
TO THIS CAREWORN FACE.
AND THO' MY STEPS GROW WEARY
AS I MAKE THE CLIMB,
STILL I HEAR YOUR MUSIC,
OH WHISPERING PINES.

(One of the SWINDLES plays the chimes.)

HAZEL. Do I hear wedding bells?

34: " THE WEDDING OF THE FLOWERS"

(RENNABELLE, AMERICA, MABEL and AZILEE assemble as the Bridesmaids. GLADYS, who has momentarily disappeared to get bridal veil and bouquet, re-enters to the strains of the "Wedding March" and proceeds to ABBOTT, who as the Groom, has donned swallowtail dinner jacket and top hat, and HAZEL, who, as Parson, holds the Bible.)

HAZEL. Dearly beloved, we are gathered together before two million radio fans to perform "The Wedding of the Flowers" a floral fantasy from the feverish feather quill of Miss Gladys Fritts. And a one, and a two, and a one, two, three...

ALL.
IF YOU LOVE THE SUNSHINE
IF YOU LOVE THE MOONSHINE
WHY, OH WHY DON'T YOU LOVE ME?
I WONDER
IF YOU LOVE THE FLOWERS
EVERY DAY FOR HOURS
WHY, OH WHY DON'T YOU LOVE ME?
SAY YOU DO, SAY YOU DO, SAY YOU DO

ABBOTT.
I DO.

ALL.
WHAT CARE I FOR HOLLYWOOD CHARMS
WHEN YOU'RE IN MY ARMS?
PARDON ME, BUTTERCUP
IF I INTERRUPT

IT COULD RAIN FOR HOURS
WHO'S AFRAID OF SHOWERS?
LONG AS I HAVE YOU LOVIN' ME

ABBOTT. He do.
GLADYS. She do.
HAZELNUTS.
DO DO DE DO

(As a button to the song, ABBOTT and GLADYS kiss loudly into the microphone.)

GLADYS. *(Overcome with emotion.)* Oh dear me, I can't bear the thought of leaving you, Hazel. We've been so close, like Mary and Martha, Ruth and Naomi.

HAZEL. Sacco and Vanzetti. Why Gladys Fritts, you silly cabbage, it's just a radio tableau. *(To EVERYONE.)* Besides, we're all going on the honeymoon with you!

AMERICA. Where to, Swami G?

GLADYS. Egypt!

35: "QUEENIE TAKE ME HOME"

GLADYS. *(Over vamp.)* We tread through the Valley of the Ancient Egyptian Kings and Queens. Suddenly we come upon a mysterious Royal Door.

(Violin makes sound of door creaking open.)

ABBOTT. We enter into Cleopatra's Crypt.

ALL. Oooo!

ABBOTT. We hoist open the granite lid to reveal the gold figure of the Queen. *(Sound of rachet.)* A strange gilded serpent is coiled around her temples.

(Sound of rattle.)

GLADYS. If only CLEO could speak, what would she say?

AMERICA. Get that snake off my head?

GLADYS. We accidentally knock our knees on the Royal Commode.

(Rim shot.)

ABBOTT. Ow!

GLADYS. And make a startling discovery...

(AMERICA squawks.)

GLADYS. There, on top, is a crumbling piece of Egyptian sheet music.

*(One of the LADIES hands ABBOTT the sheet music for "**Queenie, Take Me Home**".)*

ALL. *(To ABBOTT.)* What does it say?

ABBOTT. *(Into the microphone, like a true radio announcer.)* "Queenie, Take Me Home," a foxtrot by Garland Glenn and the Singing Pharaohs of Mobile, Alabama.

HAZEL.

QUEEN CLEOPATRA AND HER ROYAL CREW WENT
   WALKING BY THE NILE, EGYPTIAN STYLE
THEY STOPPED FOR SOME CAKE WHEN A LITTLE BITTY
   SNAKE CRAWLED OUT OF THE GRASS AND SIGHED

GLADYS, RENNABELLE and AMERICA.

"QUEENIE, TAKE ME HOME WITH YOU
QUEENIE, TAKE ME HOME WITH YOU"
THAT LITTLE ASP WAS HEARD TO GASP
"QUEENIE, TAKE ME HOME
WO-OH"
BA DA LA PA BA DA LA PA BA DA LA PA BA DA LA PA
   DO DE OH
DA DA DA DA DA DA DA DAOW!

RENNABELLE.

SHE GAVE THAT SNAKE A PRIVATE ROOM

AMERICA.

RIGHT NEXT DOOR TO KING TUT'S TOMB.

GLADYS.

SHE FED HIM GRAPES AND BARBECUE

ALL.

AND TOOK HIM FOR A RIDE IN HER TUTU.

SHE THOUGHT HE WAS HER FRIEND
SHE THOUGHT HE WAS HER FRIEND
BUT SHE GOT HAD
THAT SNAKE WENT BAD

ABBOTT, MISS MABEL, MISS AZILEE.

AND HE BIT HER IN THE END.

LADIES.

WOO!

(INSTRUMENTAL)

AMERICA and RENNABELLE.
QUEEN CLEOPATRA AND HER CRANKY OLD ASP WERE
       SMOOCHING ON THE COUCH
WHEN THE QUEEN CRIED "OUCH"
THEN THAT DIRTY LITTLE VARMINT
SLITHERED OUT OF HER GARMENT
YOU COULD BARELY HEAR HIM SAY
   GLADYS, RENNABELLE and AMERICA.
"QUEENIE, TAKE ME HOME WITH YOU
QUEENIE, TAKE ME HOME WITH YOU"
THAT LITTLE ASP WAS HEARD TO GASP
"QUEENIE, TAKE ME HOME
WO-OH!"
BA DA LA PA BA DA LA PA BA DA LA PA BA DA LA PA
      DO DE OH
DA DA DA DA DA DA DA DAOW!
   GLADYS, ABBOTT, MABEL.
QUEENIE TAKE ME HOME
   RENNABELLE, HAZEL AMERICA.
HOW COULD YOU LEAVE ME DOWN ON THE NILE
   GLADYS, ABBOTT, MABEL.
QUEENIE TAKE ME HOME
   RENNABELLE, HAZEL, AMERICA.
YA KNEW I'D FALL FOR YOUR SCHOOLGIRL SMILE
   GLADYS, RENNABELLE, HAZEL, AMERICA,
   ABBOTT, MABEL.
YA CALLED ME SWEET PATOOTIE; YOU SAID YOU'D
      BE TRUE
YA SAID THE SAME THING TO ANTONY TOO
   GLADYS, ABBOTT, MABEL.
QUEENIE TAKE ME HOME
   RENNABELLE, HAZEL, AMERICA.
I GOT AN AUGUR AND IT'S AWFUL LARGE
   GLADYS, ABBOTT, MABEL.
QUEENIE TAKE ME HOME

RENNABELLE, HAZEL, AMERICA.
I'LL BORE A HOLE IN THE SIDE OF YOUR BARGE
GLADYS, RENNABELLE, HAZEL, AMERICA,
ABBOTT, MABEL.
THEY'LL TALK ABOUT IT FROM CAIRO TO ROME
THEY'LL SAY YA SHOULDA TAKEN ME HOME
GLADYS, RENNABELLE, AMERICA SING DESCANT
while HAZEL, MABEL and ABBOTT.
YA YA YA YA YA YA YA YA YA YA YA YA
YA YA YA YA YA YA YA YA YA YA YA YA
GLADYS, RENNABELLE, HAZEL, AMERICA,
ABBOTT, MABEL.
QUEENIE TAKE ME
QUEENIE TAKE ME
QUEENIE TAKE ME HOME

HAZEL. We witness the Tragic Queen all deflated and undone. Her train of royal Courtesans disappears into the river's mist, their arguing voices fading further and further away...

(RENNABELLE and AMERICA speak the following lines at the same time, gradually fading to a whisper.)

RENNABELLE. Neja la wa hell ya, ya zena, see accola war na fiss nee na...

AMERICA. Shishkabob falafel, pita, bishka bishka boo...

HAZEL. Until there is nothing left by the Sphinx-like silence of the Spheres.

AMERICA. Goodbye, Queenie.

RENNABELLE. Farewell asp.

36: "SIGN OFF"

HAZEL. *(Over the "Sign Off" underscoring.)* And verily, in the twinkling of an eye, we are back in Cedar Ridge, where the night shall be filled with music, and the little mischiefs that deviled the day shall pack up their tents and steal away. Good night to those in the EAST, good night to those in the WEST. I hope you've enjoyed the program.

(HAZEL turns to the band and conducts as the music swells to a climax. GLADYS throws her bouquet to MISS MABEL who catches it in measure # 15. On the last chord ABBOTT and GLADYS kiss.)

END OF PLAY

COSTUME PLOT

HAZEL HUNT:
Matronly dress, perhaps a navy blue dotted Swiss or matronly flower print. Black matron shoes.

GLADYS FRITTS:
White low cut dress with triangular collar, more fashionable. White hose, white shoes with heels. A long string of beads.

O.B. ABBOTT:
Conservative period suit (w/vest, neck or bowtie) bowler hat, oxford shoes. He carries a briefcase with notepad and pencil. He may possess goggles and scarf to wear when riding his motorcycle.

AMERICA:
Flower print dress. Period hat. Black strapped shoes. White socks.

RENNABELLE:
More sophisticated in dress and behavior than America. Collared Blouse with necktie, skirt, or possibly trousers. Wears watch fob, or wristwatch. Shoes or boots.

MISS AZILEE SWINDLE:
Matronly print dress. Matron shoes.

MISS MABEL SWINDLE:
Matronly print dress. Matron shoes.

The costumes for "RADIO GALS" should reflect the period of the middle to late 1920's. And although the setting is considered rural, Hazel and her friends appreciate fine clothes and attempt to dress accordingly. Hazel and the Swindle Sisters tend to be old-fashioned in their tastes, whereas Gladys fancies herself theatrically. Rennabelle and America are, in their own fashion, more modern-style girls. Swindle sisters preferably lilac toned prints, can be complementary designs.

It should be noted that early radio performers often attempted to costume themselves for their musical and dramatic presentations, even though there was no live studio audience, for the most part. However, setting the radio scene through costumes and props seemed to inspire and enrich the imagination of both broadcaster and listener. Hazel Hunt and her Hazelnuts tend to costume their travelogues and tableaux with props they improvise from household items, or concoct out of fabric and paper and paste. This propensity is only hinted at in the prop list. It is left to the imagination and resources of each individual director, choreographer, and theater company, as to how far they want to go.

PROPERTY LIST

1 period-looking Transmitter (inoperable)—with speaker and removable knob

1 pair of headphones for transmitter

1 period Victor-style phonograph

Period looking microphones and stands (suggested: one standing microphone in front of Hazel's usual position, and one standing or hanging microphone in the band area. Depending on the sound needs of the production, these microphones could be fully wired and functional, or merely for appearance, if body mikes are used, or natural acoustics are preferred.)

Stack of period phonograph records

Telephone

Assortment of postcards and letters (see script for specifics for what cards/letters should read)

* 1 large mason jar FULL of mayonnaise

Oriental carpets (1 under drum kit; 1 under center microphone; others as needed)

* Horehound display stand with 3-5 bottles of Horehound Compound

Plain brown paper bag (for Gladys' sandwiches)

Paper wrapped sandwiches (daily perishables)

Birdwhistle

1 scrapbook full of clippings

1 newspaper

1 briefcase

Pad and pencils for briefcase

Stack of miscellaneous period sheet music, including: "Queenie Take Me Home," "Kittens in the Snow," and "Why Did You Make Me Love You" sheet music

Broadcasting License in frame

1 floorlamp with removable lamp shade

Knitting bag

Balls of yarn

Knitting needles

Clothesline

2 pairs of pinking shears

Mail bag (FULL of mail, wires, telegrams)
1 feather duster or dustcloth
Large book (Complete Works of MILTON)
Allspice jar
One bottle of smelling salts
1 musket
6 ukuleles
1 xylophone stand
1 wedding bouquet
Bible for wedding
1 duffel bag
6 or 7 pith helmets
Sisters of Pythias broaches (6)
Sandwich plate
Tray with coffee pot (with liquid), cup and saucer, spoon
Portrait of Grandpa Hunt hanging on the wall
Coffee cup for Hazel at top of show
Sofa
Hardback chair (for Abbott to get tied in to)
Arm chair
Footstool
Tall stool (for bass player) as needed
Small side table as needed for telephone
* Conducting baton

Suggested Musical Instruments: (should be period looking if possible)

Upright Piano
Drum set
Violin
Upright bass
Bflat tuba
Accordion
6 string acoustic guitar
Saxophone
Clarinet
Trumpet
Ukuleles, (5-7)

4 Orchestral chimes, midrange
    D,F, G, Bflat
Xylophone
Trombone
Banjo

RADIO GALS
Authors' suggested stage scene

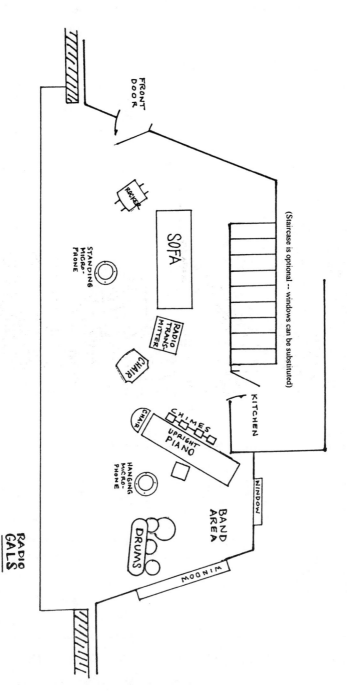

RADIO
GALS

Authors' suggested stage design

Evelyn
and the
Polka King

A play by
John Olive

Music by
Carl Finch & Bob Lucas

Lyrics by
Bob Lucas

Dethroned polka king Henry Czerniak meets Evelyn, an intense 18-year-old from Texas who has just discovered - to her horror - that Hank is her father. They pull Hank's legendary band back together and hit the road looking for Evelyn's mother. Originally commissioned by the Mad River Theatre Works in Ohio, this exuberant celebration of polka passion has been a hit at Actors Theatre of Louisville, Chicago's Steppenwolf Theatre, Pittsburgh's City Theatre and many other locations.

THE CAST
Henry, the polka king, a man in his forties or fifties
Evelyn, an intelligent, rich young lady
The Vibra-Tones, a five-piece on-stage polka band
1 additional actress to play a variety of roles

THE MUSIC
The vibrant musical numbers, the underscoring and the musical effects and transitions are in the popular polka tradition of stirring waltzes, polkas and obereks.

Terms quoted on application; music available on rental. (#7122)

Samuel French, Inc.
SERVING THE THEATRICAL COMMUNITY SINCE 1830